ROLLS-ROYCE HERITAGE TRUST

CW01085254

THE ROLLS-ROYCE
TAY ENGINE
AND THE BAC ONE-ELEVEN

Ken Goddard

HISTORICAL SERIES No 30

Published in 2000 by the
Rolls-Royce Heritage Trust
P O Box 31 Derby England DE24 8BJ

ISBN: 1 872922 19 8

The Historical Series is published as a joint initiative by the Rolls-Royce Heritage Trust, the Sir Henry Royce Memorial Foundation and the Rolls-Royce Enthusiasts' Club.

Previous volumes published in the Series are listed at the rear, together with volumes available in the Rolls-Royce Heritage Trust Technical Series.

Cover picture: Dee Howard's Tay-powered, BAC1-11 2400; first flight, 2 July 1990

Books are available from:
Rolls-Royce Heritage Trust, Rolls-Royce plc, Moor Lane, PO Box 31, Derby DE24 8BJ

Origination and reproduction by Neartone Ltd, Arnold, Nottingham
Printed by Premier Print, Glaisdale Parkway, Bilborough, Nottingham

CONTENTS

FOREWORD

Through its series of books, lectures and recordings, the Trust attempts to capture a comprehensive history of Rolls-Royce. On occasions this includes salutary lessons learned amongst the many successes achieved by the Company.

Ken Goddard is eminently well qualified to record the history of what started out as a promising combination the Tay engine and the BAC One-Eleven aeroplane. He joined the Company in 1960, initially in the Performance Department and following a short break with Vickers, subsequently in the Preliminary Design Department until 1978. Ken was then appointed a Regional Sales Manager in Marketing before moving to a Product Strategy group concentrating on the Tay engine in 1987. It was here that he became involved in the re-engining of the BAC One-Eleven, a programme which eventually came to nought, but the experience of which was useful in the subsequent successful launch of the Tay re-engining of the Boeing 727-100 package freighters.

Ken was appointed Head of Marketing for Small Engines in 1994, retired at the end of 1996 and, in retirement, produced the manuscript for this book before the history was lost. We are grateful to him.

Richard Haigh
February 2001

PREFACE

It was during a filing cabinet clear-out in the Marketing Department of Rolls-Royce, in 1996, that the idea for this booklet was born. We had come across a number of files about the Tay/BAC One-Eleven project and it occurred to me that some years hence, people might say, "I wonder what happened to that Tay-engined One-Eleven? It seemed like a good idea at the time."

The concept of fitting new, quiet, fuel-efficient, Rolls-Royce Tay engines to the popular but noisy and inefficient British Aircraft Corporation One-Eleven 100-seat commercial airliner was so obviously right that the enthusiasm for the project in its early days seemed well justified. Sadly, and notwithstanding the successful flying of two Tay/One-Eleven prototypes, the promise was not fulfilled. Over a period of eleven years several other attempts were made to launch a Tay/One-Eleven programme. This is an attempt to record the story.

My personal interest in the programme began in about 1987, when I became informally associated with the Tay Project, although I recall being vigorously lectured on the subject by Derek Lowe at the 1984 Hannover Airshow. As time went on I became actively involved, first in marketing the concept with the Dee Howard Company and later in discussions with the Romanians. Thus in 1996, with my interest in the subject still strong, I saved as many files as I could from incineration and started to write this little monograph.

Although Rolls-Royce is arguably the United Kingdom's premier engineering company I apologise to my fellow engineers that this booklet is not much of an engineering text but more of a tale of management (or mismanagement!), company strategies, internal politics, missed opportunities, hidden agendas and for good measure, Romanian ambitions. But perhaps more than anything else, it is an attempt to set down the sad story of a luckless piece of aviation history, which promised so much.

I should warn that I have made no attempt to chronicle the actual launch of the Tay engine, which was somewhat controversial, nor the development of the engine itself, which took place primarily at Rolls-Royce's East Kilbride factory in Scotland. There are a number of distinguished and talented staff around who were involved with the development of the programme and its successful application to the Gulfstream IV, Fokker 70 and 100 and Boeing 727-100 re-engining projects and they are far more qualified than me to present the complete picture.

As readers will quickly discover the whole programme to apply the Tay engine to the One-Eleven was riddled with 'politics' and mistrust. The re-engining programme started by the Dee Howard Company (later taken over by Aeritalia) ended in 1991, in rancour and four lawsuits. This loss of the re-engining programme and the technology which it spawned was also a serious blow to the Romanians who, over a period of 10 years, tried to launch a programme for fitting the Tay engine rather than the Spey, on new production One-Elevens being built by them under licence on their Bucharest production line. Sadly, and despite a last serious effort in 1993, this programme also failed.

The main source of archive for this booklet has been a miscellany of Rolls-Royce files on the programme, supplemented by my recollections of working on the project for about seven years and much strengthened by valuable conversation and correspondence with a number of people associated with the project.

However, it is a major shortcoming that I have had only limited access to outside material. In the case of Dee Howard and Aeritalia (the latter being later renamed as Alenia), which lost a substantial amount of money in trying to launch the re-engining programme, it quickly became apparent to me that the project was now regarded as an embarrassment to be forgotten and I had no wish to stir up resentment in raising the subject. It was also seen to be very career-limiting for any Dee Howard current employee to talk about it. Further, most of the company's Tay/One-Eleven data was either in the hands of the company's lawyers or sealed away in a security store. However, I was able to obtain some useful recollections from discussions with Messrs D U Howard and Wayne Fagan and some others.

A small handful of other people who were significantly involved with the Tay/One Eleven, including a key player with British Aerospace, were unwilling to reply to my request for their comments. In the light of this and the perceptions that I had formed, I decided not to seek a corporate view on the programme from British Aerospace. BAe's stance on this programme is surmised by various other parties in the text.

The section of this monograph dealing with the aftermath of the Dee Howard programme has been rather difficult to write. When Alenia decided to terminate the re-engining programme, because it could see no likely return on its investment, four lawsuits were launched, one by Alenia itself and the others by three parties which had been disadvantaged by the termination. Three of the four cases were settled out of court and it has been almost impossible to ascertain the nature of the settlements, or anybody willing to talk about them. Two of the lawsuits were filed at the Bexar County Court in San Antonio, which was quite unwilling to communicate with me, and I was only able to learn anything about these cases when the chance opportunity occurred to re-visit San Antonio, Texas, where the Dee Howard Company is based.

One major problem on the Rolls-Royce side is that I have not been able to track down a single surviving copy of the daily and weekly reports written by Jon Taylor and others in Rolls-Royce's office in San Antonio on the conduct of the Dee Howard flight test programme. Most of the copies went to addressees in Tay Engineering and Product Support in East Kilbride but when that department sadly closed down in 1995/96, none of the files seemed to survive the relocation to Derby. Even the originating office's copy was later scrapped.

Reflecting on data sources generally it is fortunate that the events described in this story mostly took place in the era when hard copies of communications were sent and filed. In today's scenario, where so much information is sent by e-mail, much of the internal correspondence which is so valuable to amplify a story would probably have only a short life in PC hard drive and then erased.

Overshadowing the attempts to fit the Tay engine on Romania's One-Eleven was the matter of the Romanian Spey Licence Agreement and attempts to convert it into a Tay Agreement. I have decided not to delve into the subject of Licence Agreements. This particular area of the Rolls-Royce's commercial business is a complex, arcane and difficult subject and envelopes the staff involved in years of traumatic negotiation and need for great patience. Since the Tay was not licensed in Romania it is convenient not to deal with it, but this subject of licensing is important and deserves a separate commentary, by one of its experts, in another document.

Acknowledgements

In helping me to prepare this little booklet, a large number of people have been very generous with their time and support. I have already mentioned Dee U Howard and Wayne Fagan. Also outside Rolls-Royce I should like to thank Ian Munro, partner of the late Salem Binladen in Salian Ltd, Roger Back, formerly BAe's Chief Engineer for the One-Eleven programme, Brian Kyme, formerly Managing Director of Associated Aerospace, Derek Lowe, then Director of Executive Jet Sales, Max Bacon, who was with Marshall's of Cambridge, Ed Searle of Lovaux, later with FLS, Captain Ed Halscheid, who was Chief Pilot and Manager of the Flight Department of HM Industies, Dr Ken Holden formerly of GPA, Douglas Harpley formerly of Turbo-Union and several staff members of the current Dee Howard Company.

Among a number of Rolls-Royce employees, or retired employees, I should like to highlight both for his work on the Tay and his advice on this booklet, Norman Wilson, Tay Chief Engineer, and include thanks for the support of his successor, Frank Reford. I must also thank quite a number of former colleagues for their help in a variety of ways, including (in alphabetical order), John M Charlton, Ty Farquhar, Peter Hopkins, Ian

Kinnear, Dr David Mitchell, Mike G Scott, Paul Simpkin, Jonathan Taylor, Stan Todd, Jan Turnbull, and many good friends in the Tay Project and Marketing Departments. I am grateful for their advice and recollections and for a wide area of help with business and technical data. I must also offer thanks for information and publishing assistance from Luisa Bollard, Sue Bristow, Clive Crocker and Roger C Taylor and mention particularly the generous help with software and PC support from Michael N Holmes. Finally, it is also fitting that I should remember here, with sadness, the late Stan Birch, a good friend and Tay Project Sales Engineer and the late Peter Armstrong, Head of Marketing, who were both active with the Tay One-Eleven in the early days of the programme.

Often in large organisations, hard-working team members make significant achievements but rarely see their names or responsibilities in print. In an attempt to highlight those who managed various Tay activities, I have attempted in Appendix III to recall and record the composition of the Tay Project management teams in 1988 and 1990, both key years in the Tay chronology. Inevitably, I may have accidentally left of some important contributors, or have given people wrong titles. My apologies to all concerned for such errors.

To Rolls-Royce plc itself I should like to give thanks for the use of a number of photographs and charts kindly supplied by the Marketing and Photographic Departments.

I should also like to acknowledge the help of the Editor-in-Chief of *Flight International* for permission to reproduce a number of items from the journal and the magnificent cutaway drawing and the Editor of the *Derby Evening Telegraph* for permission to reproduce an item from his paper.

Finally, I should like to thank the Officers of the Rolls-Royce Heritage Trust for their encouragement in my writing this booklet.

Notes on layout and nomenclature etc

This story of the Tay and the One-Eleven has been laid out in broadly a chronological fashion. For reference purposes a brief chronological table has been set out in Appendix I.

In all references to the aircraft I have used the words 'One-Eleven' as employed by BAC/BAe in its literature. The only exception is in mention of the Dee Howard aircraft, or in Dee Howard's published material, where the abbreviated '1-11' was used.

I have generally shortened the title British Aerospace to BAe, as widely used. In the case of the re-engining programme I have used either the name, The Dee Howard Company or, as often shortened, Dee Howard. If I mention Mr D U Howard, I am referring specifically to the founder and owner of the original company.

As regards engine designations, somebody will point out that the proper title for the engine subject of this booklet is Tay Mark 650 engine, but in all cases I have abbreviated the designation to Tay 650.

Ken Goddard
Derby, England
2000

THE TAY ENGINE
AND THE BAC ONE-ELEVEN

CHAPTER ONE

The British Aircraft Corporation One-Eleven Aircraft

The British Aircraft Corporation's One-Eleven civil jet airliner was one of Great Britain's most successful post-World War II civil aircraft projects. The concept was for a fast, ie jet-powered, regional airliner of at least 70 seats which would have high productivity and a number of features to reduce turn-round time at airports. The aircraft was intended to succeed the popular Viscount turboprop-powered aircraft, of which over 400 had been built. The aircraft was produced in five versions and 235 were constructed, not including those manufactured under licence in Romania. All were powered by various versions of the low bypass ratio Rolls-Royce Spey engine, named like a number of Rolls-Royce aero engines, after a river.

The initial version, the -200 Series, was ordered off the drawing board by British United Airways in May 1961 and was followed by several orders from US airlines, the first being from Braniff International Airways in October. The first prototype flew on 28 August 1963, the type received its Certificate of Airworthiness on 6 April 1965 and entered service on 9 April 1965. Note that the BAC One-Eleven's main competitor, the DC9, first entered service in December 1965, eight months later.

The first One-Eleven for Braniff International Airways taking off

After the -200 Series, of which 58 ultimately were built, only a handful of the -300 Series were produced and the next major development was the -400 Series, for which a launch order for 15 firm plus 15 option aircraft was awarded by American Airlines in July 1963. This variant had the same dimensions as the -200 Series but was cleared to higher weights and powered by more powerful Spey 511 engines.

The last major production variant was the -500 Series, which had an increase of fuselage length and extended wingtips and could seat 97-119 passengers, according to airline specification. It entered service with British Airways on 7 November 1968. The power for this heavier weight aircraft came from a further development of the Spey engine, the Spey 512-14DW.

One other variant of the One-Eleven which is of particular interest is the -475 Series, of which 10 were built. This combined the bigger wing of the -500 Series with the shorter fuselage of the -400 Series. The improved performance standard offered by this combination, together with a number of other changes, was targetted at customers who wanted short airfield, high rate-of-climb operations out of little-prepared airstrips.

A chart summarising the One-Eleven family is shown below.

BAC One-Eleven variants

Series	-200	-300	-400	-475	-500
Number produced	58	9	70	12	86
Dimensions (ft)					
Overall length	93.5	93.5	93.5	93.5	107
Wing Span	88.5	88.5	88.5	93.6	93.6
Weights (lb)-					
Max Take-Off	79,000	87,500	87,500-89,500	98,500	99,650-104,500
Max Zero Fuel	64,000	71,000	72,000	73,000	81,000
Max Payload	16,850	18,200	19,200	19,200	24,600
Number of seats	69-84	69-89	69-89	69-89	97-119

Propelled by President Ceaucescu's potent political desire for a Romanian aerospace industry that was able to produce aircraft which could sell in the West, the Romanian Import/Export agency signed a licence agreement with British Aerospace in 1978, for the Romanians to take over new production of the One-Eleven 500 Series and produce up to 50 aircraft. The new aircraft would be sold under the brand name ROMBAC One-Eleven. Assembly of the first 22 was to be from parts supplied by BAe, with an increasing content of Romanian built parts. The first Romanian-assembled aircraft flew on 18 September 1982.

Roll-out of the first ROMBAC One-Eleven

However, by the time of signature of the Romanian Licence Agreement, noise and combustion emissions legislation was in the offing which would have the effect of exposing the high level of these environmental pollutants on the One-Eleven and harm the potential for sales of the aircraft in the West. In fact, any new design of commercial transport aircraft certificated after October 1977 would have to meet the new Chapter 3 noise levels recommended by the International Civil Aviation Organisation and Stage 3 levels proposed by the Federal Aviation Authority in the USA. The hush-kitted, Spey-powered, BAC One-Eleven could barely meet the higher Chapter 2 noise limits. In other words, the Romanian-assembled aircraft would suffer an increasing marketing disadvantage against new competing aircraft.

Likewise on combustion emissions, ICAO was already discussing the establishment of regulations to limit the levels of four pollutants, unburnt hydrocarbons, carbon monoxide, oxides of nitrogen and smoke. These regulations did not actually come into effect until 1986 and were not retroactive, but nevertheless pointed up the fact that, against its new competitors the One-Eleven, with its relatively 'dirty' Spey engines, was going to be somewhat at a disadvantage.

The Romanians realised this and it was, therefore, spelt out in the Co-operation Agreements between the various parties that British Aerospace and Rolls-Royce would vigorously pursue technologies which would reduce aircraft noise and emissions.

13

BAC One-Eleven product developments with derivatives of the Spey engine

Following the launch of the improved versions of the BAC One-Eleven, the -400, the -475 and the -500, project work continued at the British Aircraft Corporation on further developments of this popular aircraft. There were several proposals, called variously -600, -670 and -700 and the history of BAC's various One-Eleven proposals and associated derivatives of the Spey engine which complemented the aircraft, are worthy of a chapter, possibly even a booklet, on their own, but unfortunately will not be pursued here.

In 1974, particular effort was put into trying to launch the One-Eleven 700. This variant was to have had a 12ft (3.66m) longer fuselage than the -500, a take-off weight increased from 104,500lb to 117,000lb and an increase from 119 to 134 passengers, depending on cabin arrangements, seat pitching etc. The power plant proposed for this development was called the 'Re-fanned Spey' and given the designation Spey 67C or Spey Mk 606.

In layout the Spey 606 was a precursor of the Tay engine, to be launched later (in 1983) and had a large single stage fan and a bypass ratio of nearly 2.0 to 1, compared with the 0.7 ratio of the Spey 512-14 in the -500 Series aircraft. The Spey 606 was somewhat larger than the Tay, having a take-off thrust of 16,900lbf and a fan diameter of 46.9 inches (119.1 cm). Like the later Tay, the single-stage fan was coupled to a three-stage Intermediate Pressure (IP) compressor in the core airflow and driven by a new three-stage Low Pressure (LP) turbine. BAC marketed this aircraft but crucially failed to gain the selection of British Airways.

On 1 January 1978, the British Aircraft Corporation amalgamated with Hawker-Siddeley Aviation to become British Aerospace (BAe).

In 1977-78 BAe and Rolls-Royce were active on yet another proposed version of the One-Eleven, -600 Series, this having a further development of the Spey called the Mk 514 and coupled with a translating shroud ejector silencer attached to the engine. This was a BAe attempt to try to meet the obligations in its forthcoming Romanian licence to find noise reductions for the aircraft. British Airways was not particularly interested in this and opted instead to purchase Boeing 737 aircraft, which started to be delivered in late 1979.

There were further proposals for One-Eleven developments, with even more change to the airframe and powered by engines far bigger than the Spey or Tay, but these proposals are far beyond the scope of this volume.

Interest in an improved version of the BAC One-Eleven aircraft, with quieter, more efficient engines, resumed in the latter part of 1982. Rolls-Royce was then working on a new proposal, the 'Hi Flow Spey', RB183-03, a development of the existing RB183 version of the Spey which was the engine in the Fokker F28 aircraft. The Hi Flow Spey had a new, higher bypass ratio, single-stage fan and was being offered for an improved Fokker F28. However, the Chairman of Gulfstream Aerospace, Allen Paulson, saw the potential of the Hi Flow Spey as a powerplant for his next generation Gulfstream business jet, the Gulfstream IV. Publicity by Paulson in the magazine *Aviation Week & Space Technology* triggered a number of enquiries by American corporate operators of the One-Eleven -400 Series aircraft to British Aerospace's Washington office.

The Weybridge division of BAe, which had become somewhat dispirited by its failure to launch any of the derivatives of the One-Eleven on which it had been working for so many years, was heartened by this interest. Although new production of One-Elevens had already switched to Romania, BAe saw an opportunity of being able to offer re-engining the One-Eleven for greater range, such that with the more efficient engines and extra, long range tanks, the aircraft would have a range of 3400 nautical miles, including reserves, ie transatlantic capability.

However, with the level of thrust being offered at the time, the aircraft was marginal at meeting the new Federal Aircraft Regulation, Part 36, Stage 3 and ICAO Chapter 3 noise regulations at the flyover condition.

At a meeting with Rolls-Royce on the project in September 1982, BAe drew attention again to the fact that in the terms of its licence agreement with the Romanian Aircraft Factory, it was obliged to tell the Romanians of any proposed developments of the One-Eleven. Of particular interest would be any developments which improved the competitiveness of the aircraft and reduced the noise and combustor emissions. The possible introduction of a much quieter engine, to be called the Tay, was clearly a major contribution which could be offered.

Coincidentally the Romanians had sent a notice that it wished to discontinue the use of the noisy Spey engine on their One-Eleven -500 Series aircraft after Ship Number 12. As noted earlier, the first Romanian-built One-Eleven had flown in September that year (1982).

It is also interesting to note that at this time, in an off-the-record telephone conversation between a senior BAe Engineer and his Rolls-Royce contact, it was explained that the official internal BAe position about the Tay and the One-Eleven was that *"nothing must be done to harm the BAe 146"*. (BAe's new principal product, the four-engined 100-seater which was about the same size as the One-Eleven). We will become aware of this attitude again later in the narrative.

Launch of the Tay engine

The RB183-03 engine was officially launched in the Gulfstream IV in January 1983 and became known as the Tay Mark 610-8, or Tay 610-8. The engine comprised the core or HP system of the Spey RB183 Mark 555-15 engine (the most reliable version of the Spey), a new single-stage fan of 44 inches (111.8 cm) diameter, a new three-stage IP compressor and a new three-stage LP turbine. Nominal Maximum Take-Off thrust of this initial variant was 12,420 lbf.

The Fokker Company launched its F28 replacement aircraft, the Fokker 100, a few months after Gulfstream IV. For this application the take-off thrust of the Tay was increased to 13,850 lbf. Relative to the Spey engine it succeeded, the new Tay engine offered a substantial improvement in performance, with 10-20% increase in take-off thrust relative to the various versions of the Spey it replaced and a 20% reduction in engine specific fuel consumption. These engine improvements are shown in the following pages and aircraft performance is discussed in Chapter Five. The Tay's much higher bypass ratio (3.0 versus 0.7) resulted in a much lower core jet velocity and substantially lower noise - a key parameter for the Tay.

A considerable debate and evaluation took place about the provision of a

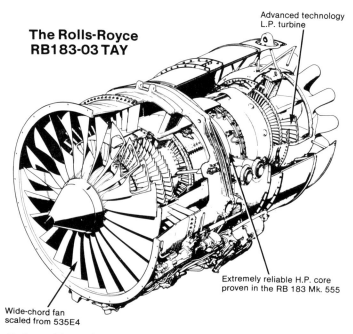

The Rolls-Royce
RB183-03 TAY

Advanced technology
L.P. turbine

Extremely reliable H.P. core
proven in the RB 183 Mk. 555

Wide-chord fan
scaled from 535E4

The Rolls-Royce Tay engine

nacelle for the Tay. Rolls-Royce management had decided that it was so committed on other engineering projects, such as the RB211-535, that it did not have the resources to undertake a nacelle development and certification programme. Accordingly the programme was put out to bids and of the six or seven received, those shortlisted were from Grumman, Shorts and Rohr. Eventually Grumman was selected, a decision which was supported by both Gulfstream and Fokker. The Spey's existing cascade thrust reverser and jet pipe was replaced by a target-type reverser.

For the Tay installation on the One-Eleven aircraft, the weight of the aircraft with its bigger engines and bigger nacelles was expected to increase by about 1,250 lb. On new Romanian-built -500 Series aircraft this increase was not expected to effect the aircraft weight distribution. However, the British Airways One-Eleven aircraft were balanced differently and it was thought that there would be a need for up to 900 lb ballast in the aircraft nose. There will be a more detailed description of the Tay installation in Chapter Five.

A chronology of the Tay engine programme, with particular respect to its installation in the One-Eleven aircraft, is shown in Appendix I.

Spey and Tay engines for the BAC One-Eleven

The table below shows a comparison of some parameters for the new Tay-powered version of the One-Eleven -500 compared with the existing Spey-powered aircraft and the earlier One-Eleven -700 project of 1974.

Variant	-500 in service	-700 1974 project	-500 + Tay 1983
Engine Type	Spey 512-14	Spey 606	Tay 612-14
Aircraft Weight (lb) at max take-off	104,500	117,000	104,500
Number of seats	99-119	119-134	99-119
Engine Thrust (lbf) at max take-off	12,550	16,900	13,850
Bypass Ratio	0.7	1.96	3.0
Fan Diameter (inches)	32.5	46.9	44.0

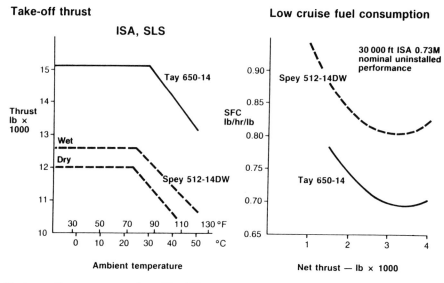

Engine performance comparison: Tay 650 versus Spey 512-14DW

Why new engines for the BAC One-Eleven?

The existing Spey-powered One-Eleven had two major disadvantages in the market place. It was very noisy - one of the noisiest of all twin-engined jet airliners - and it had a relatively high fuel consumption. Both these disadvantages stemmed from the Spey engine. Its low bypass ratio - the ratio of the amount of airflow bypassing the hot core section to that going through the core itself - resulted in a high jet velocity flow issuing from the high temperature core, the shearing effect of this high jet velocity being the fundamental contributor of jet noise. The high fuel consumption also resulted from the inefficient low bypass ratio configuration.

Switching to the high bypass ratio, high-efficiency Tay solved all these problems and resulted in about 15 percent lower fuel consumption and noise levels which would allow the One-Eleven comfortably to meet the Stage 3/Chapter 3 noise limits. The engine also offered better thrust at almost all take-off and flight conditions than the Spey 512-14DW in the BAC One-Eleven -500 Series aircraft. Another factor was that the Spey engine, particularly the Spey 512 version in the One-Eleven -500 Series, had relatively high maintenance costs (usually expressed as a dollar-per-hour rate). The Tay engine was expected to have an hourly cost rate about half that of the Spey 512.

Thus despite the capital cost of investing in a pair of new engines, there appeared to be a strong economic case for Tay re-engining. This will be discussed in Chapter Five.

For the various One-Elevens fitted out for the transportation of company executives and VIPs and carrying a light payload, the principal advantage of re-engining - in addition to the noise reduction - was that the improved fuel consumption would offer a significant increase in range and on long flights a reduced number of landings for refuelling.

The Romanians were not slow to appreciate that the newly-launched Tay engine, when installed in their new production One-Eleven -500 Series aircraft would dramatically improve the capability of those aircraft. Accordingly in May, Mr Zanfirescu, Director General of the Foreign Trade Company, Centrul National Aeronautic (CNA) wrote to the Deputy Chairman of Rolls-Royce, Don Pepper, with some ambitious proposals. In addition to his wish for the aircraft factory, Intreprinderea de Avioane Bucuresti (IAvB) to obtain the airframe and technology rights for the production of Tay nacelles, Zanfirescu wished to change the terms of the Spey 512 Licence Agreement with Rolls-Royce to allow the Romanian engine factory, Intreprindera Turbomecanica Bucuresti (ITmB) to produce Tay parts and tools. CNA also wanted Rolls-Royce to supply some Tay engines on a 'free loan' such that they could be *"fixed on a BAC One-Eleven aircraft, retrofitted by IAvB for checks and demonstrations"*. CNA also wanted Romania to become a second source for certain Tay modules.

How Rolls-Royce responded to this ambitious proposal is not recalled but the Romanian's enthusiasm was dampened somewhat when they found out that the Tay was developed around the smaller core of the Spey 555 engine rather than the larger and totally different core of the Spey 512. The latter was the Spey variant of their own One-Elevens of which they had both experience and a significant inventory of spare parts and tools.

At this time of the Tay launch, the existing Spey licence was already proving difficult to administer and the Romanian requirements for offset were difficult to fulfil. The general theme of subsequent Rolls-Royce negotiations with CNA and its successor, over many years, was to try to avoid any ITmB involvement in the Tay programme.

19

British Aerospace marketing of a Tay/One-Eleven programme

In mid-March 1983 a senior level review meeting on the Tay/One-Eleven was held between Rolls-Royce and BAe at Weybridge. Despite the fact that this was not new production aircraft business the Weybridge team was pushing the concept vigorously. Rolls-Royce had private reservations as to whether this enthusiasm was shared by the BAe corporate management and in particular the Hatfield Division, formerly Hawker-Siddeley, which was totally committed to the new BAe146 aircraft.

In July 1983 BAe sent a letter to all operators of One-Elevens, outlining the advantages and cost of re-engining the aircraft. It was apparent that BAe considered that it would undertake the certification programme and estimated a certification, ie non-recurring, cost of $25m, for covering both the -400 Series and -500 series. BAe estimated a unit price, for each aircraft converted, of about $5.5m. BAe intended to buy nacelles and thrust reversers from Grumman, although Fokker, which had a power of veto on the use of the nacelle, was not comfortable about this, seeing a threat of the re-engined aircraft to the new Fokker 100 airliner. British Aerospace saw it as key to the programme launch to try to capture the business of re-engining the -500 Series aircraft with the UK airlines British Airways (BA), British Caledonian (BCal) and Dan-Air. These UK operators did not initially appear to be particularly enthusiastic in the proposal. Separately, BAe made an unsolicited proposal to sell 12 -500 Series aircraft, re-engined with Tays, to the American airline USAir.

BAe had estimated that it needed about 35 conversions to be undertaken in order to cover the cost of the development and certification process. When, towards the end of the year insufficient interest had been shown in the offer letter, BAe withdrew the letter, probably under pressure from the Hatfield representatives on the Board, who were anxious that BAe activity should not be deflected from the need to sell more 146 aircraft which were being built at the Hatfield factory.

Despite withdrawal of the BAe offer letter, interest in the One-Eleven had been kindled and in December 1983 an enthusiastic letter was received by BAe's Sales Manager from Sir Gordon White, Chairman of Hanson Industries Inc of the USA, which owned an executive One-Eleven.

The Dee Howard Company

With the BAe offer withdrawn, a group of Middle-Eastern owners and operators of One-Elevens which had been fitted in executive configuration, led by Sheikh Salem Binladen, looked elsewhere for a company to upgrade their aircraft by re-engining. It was the Dee Howard Company of San

Antonio, Texas, which was approached by Binladen to launch the programme.

This company had been formed by Mr Durrell ('Dee') U Howard in 1947 and specialised in innovative aircraft engineering and modification programmes and employed about 1000 people, with a large contingent of qualified engineers and designers. The company had also bought the rights to a very promising thrust reverser design and had developed a significant capability in nacelle and thrust reverser design and manufacture.

Mr Howard had already formed a business relationship with Sheikh Binladen, both as a result of work done on Sheikh Binladen's Lear Jet and because of the company's work on customising a Boeing 747 for the Saudi royal family. The latter programme was signed in May 1983 and work started at the end of that year. Salem Binladen was a son of a Saudi family which owned a large trading company and at the time owned a -400 Series executive One-Eleven. Sheikh Binladen was concerned to operate over longer ranges and reduce the number of refuelling stops. The big increase in range offered by Tay re-engining would be ideal for him.

Supporting Sheikh Binladen during these early discussions was Ian Munro, Binladen's representative in London. For the purposes of launching the re-engine business of Binladen with the Dee Howard Company, Munro established a company called Salian, registered in London. Munro claimed a significant role in drawing British Aerospace and Rolls-Royce into the proposed re-engining programme. BAe held the design rights for the One-Eleven and no re-design of the aircraft for re-engining could take place without BAe's approval. Terms of Agreement between Salian and the Dee Howard Company were negotiated progressively throughout 1985. They had the effect of establishing a series of rights and obligations between the two companies and recognised Salian's role in negotiating agreements with BAe and Rolls-Royce.

Before the Dee Howard Company could proceed with the re-engining programme it needed a significant amount of data and technical support from British Aerospace. During the negotiations to secure this data, conducted principally by Mr Howard's personal counsel, Wayne Fagan, and supported by Tom Finch, VP for Engineering, British Aerospace made it a condition of granting a licence or Technical Assistance Agreement that Dee Howard must negotiate with the Romanians for the latter to have access to the Tay installation technology for their new aircraft programme. Wayne Fagan claims that BAe informed the Romanians of this pre-condition and suggests that this loaded the negotiating scales against Dee Howard.

Quite separate from these difficulties, it was apparent to outsiders that the bilateral negotiations between Dee Howard and BAe itself were protracted and time-consuming. In retrospect both Ian Munro and Wayne Fagan described the process as particularly tiresome and difficult. There seemed to be a total lack of interest by British Aerospace and the only thing which focused BAe's attention was its contractual commitments to the Romanians. Ian Munro found it necessary to make a great many visits to Bucharest to encourage the Romanians to put pressure on BAe to support the potential improvements to the One-Eleven. Munro felt obliged to point out that the aircraft had no future without Tay engines.

A consequence of the discussions between Dee Howard and Ian Munro was to raise Romanian ambitions for a Tay-powered ROMBAC aircraft such that several articles about such a programme appeared in the aviation press in early 1985. It is worth recording that senior officials of the UK Government's Department of Trade & Industry (DTI) and notably Mr Kester George, asked Wayne Fagan to keep them informed of progress with his negotiations with the Romanians. This was because the Government-backed Export Credit Guarantee Department had guaranteed the financing of the Romanian One-Eleven (Spey) programme and the DTI wished to keep an eye on its commitment.

In order to facilitate the launch of the programme a contract was required between Rolls-Royce and the Dee Howard Company for the supply of Tay engines. Rolls-Royce required an advance payment of £995,030 but DHC claimed not to be financially capable of meeting this demand and Sheikh Binladen was persuaded to put up this money from his personal funds. Sheikh Binladen also guaranteed a bank loan of £1m to the Dee Howard Company, as working capital, a loan which was subsequently repaid.

It is interesting to note that Rolls-Royce's name does not appear much in the reporting of the Dee Howard launch negotiations. Reading between the lines one gets the impression that the company did not see re-engining as a major programme, nor did it see much of a market. With the Gulfstream IV and Fokker 100 programmes already launched and viewed as much more important, there seems to have been a feeling of letting Dee Howard and BAe get on with it.

Initial attempts to launch a British re-engine programme

Meanwhile, one of the first to recognise the potential benefits of re-engining the One-Eleven was Derek Lowe, Director of the UK company Executive Jet Sales. Derek had been successful in selling used BAC One-Eleven and HS125 aircraft and had promoted and sold HS125s re-engined with Garrett TFE 731 engines.

In 1982 Derek had examined the possibilities for improving the range capability of the Spey-powered One-Eleven -475 and -500 Series aircraft for possible long range executive operations on direct routes such as Jeddah-

London and Lagos-London by adding an extra conformal tank system. This appeared to be entirely practical and the resulting enhanced long range capability enabled Derek, acting as BAe's consultant, to sell the last two new British-built One-Eleven's (-475 Series) for VIP operations, with the extra tanks designed, manufactured and installed at Cranfield College of Aeronautics (now Cranfield University).

Derek recognised that maximising the fuel capacity of the One-Eleven -500 Series, whilst utilising the reduced fuel consumption of the newly-announced Tay engine, was the key to offering a full transatlantic capability for the corporate market. He considered that the -500 Series was more suitable for re-engining than the -400 (being considered by the Dee Howard Company) because of its better payload/range, its younger airframes and because its operating weights could accommodate the heavier Tay engine without penalty. Further, the improved payload/range would be more attractive to airlines and freight operators, who would be more likely to provide the larger orders that were needed to launch the programme.

After BAe withdrew its 1983 offer letter, Derek Lowe ascertained from inside sources that most interest in the re-engining concept among airlines had been shown by Peter Villa of British Island Airways (BIA) and Dan-Air and there were encouraging noises from other operators. However, finding cash to launch the programme was the largest single problem and Derek decided to approach Hanson Trust (which had for some time operated a One-Eleven). Hanson Trust showed immediate interest and indicated a willingness to arrange financing for the first 25 conversions. Moreover, on 1 July 1985, Lord Hanson wrote to Sir Austin Pearce, then Chairman of BAe to propose a meeting between BAe and Air Hanson to discuss these proposals. Either unaware of Lord Hanson's letter or deliberately ignoring it, the following day the Marketing Director of BAe wrote to Derek Lowe saying, among other things, *"We cannot generate any enthusiasm anywhere in the Corporation concerning the prospect of re-engining the 1-11 (sic) with the Tay"*. And this was at a time when BAe commercial staff were negotiating a contract with the Dee Howard Company!

Nevertheless Hanson personnel subsequently visited BAe (but without Derek Lowe) to understand the original manufacturer's position, but were thoroughly deflated by BAe's lack of interest or support.

This setback effectively deprived Derek of funding and a UK launch base. This was a serious setback, made more unfortunate by the fact that the Dee Howard Company, which was pre-occupied with commercial discussions over its proposal to launch a programme with Sheikh Binladen, had shown no interest in the UK fleets. Derek Lowe admits in retrospect that he had not appreciated how negative was the BAe corporate view on Tay re-engining. Notwithstanding the marketing benefits which had been recognised from the

HS125 re-engine programme, this must be seen as an early indication that BAe were going to be unhelpful to any prolonging of the life of the One-Eleven which would harm the prospects for the BAe 146 project.

This raises a general question about re-engining; what are the requirements for launching and completing a successful re-engining programme? The author, after some years of study and project work on aircraft re-engining, had identified seven criteria which seemed necessary to be met, to give a likelihood of success - a sort of 'litmus test'. Five of the six re-engining programmes prior to the One-Eleven, and particularly the Cammacorp DC8 programme, had met all the criteria.

Two of the seven criteria were (a) that the programme should have the support of the original aircraft manufacturer and (b) that the programme should be managed by a credible organisation. In the respect that Derek Lowe did not have BAe's support and had not yet assembled a visible project management team to run a One-Eleven -500 programme, his chances of success were not likely to be good.

CHAPTER TWO

Launch of the Dee Howard re-engining programme

The Dee Howard Company programme to re-engine the BAC One-Eleven aircraft with Rolls-Royce Tay engines was formally launched on 28 January 1986 and publicly announced in March. The development and certification aircraft, a -400 Series aircraft, was expected to fly in July 1987 and the type to receive an FAA Certificate in December 1987. (The aircraft in question, BAe Constructor Number 059, which had first entered service with American Airlines in 1966 and subsequently converted to executive configuration, had been bought by River City Investments, a company wholly owned by Mr Dee U Howard, in January 1985). Note that this launch was about two years after the Dee Howard Company started discussions with BAe on this programme.

The nature of the launch was that the Dee Howard Company had entered into a Technical Assistance Agreement with British Aerospace, whereby BAe would provide technical assistance for the FAA and CAA certification of not only the -400 Series aircraft, but also the -475 and -500 Series as well. However, the inclusion of the latter two variants was not revealed at the time. Confirmation was given that discussions had also taken place with the Romanian aircraft industry and foreign trade organisation about changing to Tay power for the new production BAC One-Eleven -560 Series aircraft which were already being built under licence in Romania. It was projected that the price per aircraft of re-engining would be about $6.5m. Financing of the programme was not announced but had been expected to come privately from Sheikh Salem Binladen. In the event it became clear that most was going to have to come from Dee Howard's own internal sources.

The Tay engine variant was to be known as the Tay 612-14 and would have the same thrust rating and virtually the same configuration as the Tay 620-15 in the Fokker 100 aircraft, with a maximum static take-off thrust on an ISA day of 13,850 pounds. Certification of the Tay 612 engine was expected to be at the end of April 1987. (This compares with the Tay 620's expected certification in June 1986). However, at the first three-way co-ordination meeting in late March (Dee Howard/BAe/Rolls-Royce), the BAe delegation, while showing noticeable enthusiasm for the project wished that Rolls-Royce had offered an increased thrust version of the Tay engine. (The Tay 650 engine, with higher thrust levels, including a take-off thrust of 15,100 lbf at sea level, had been launched with the USAir order for heavier weight Fokker 100 aircraft in July 1985).

The Dee Howard Company held a Symposium for -400 Series executive operators in San Antonio in April 1986. Representatives of nine owners attended. It was noteworthy that the Dee Howard presentation highlighted the active participation in the re-engining programme by British Aerospace and its responsibility for supplying a large amount of data and undertaking certain tests. The target date for obtaining a Supplemental Type Certificate (STC) was now given as April 1988. The improvement in aircraft fuel burn for the Tay-powered aircraft, relative to the original Spey-powered aircraft was very significant and quoted as between 15-20%. In response to a question about price, Dee Howard quoted $6.75m for each of the first five conversions.

Continuing talks about a British re-engine programme

Notwithstanding the announcement of the Dee Howard programme launch, apparently centred on the -400 Series executive aircraft, Derek Lowe continued to try to attract support for a separate UK-based programme to re-engine the -500 Series One-Eleven and engaged in increasingly strident correspondence with the senior Directors of British Aerospace, with Rolls-Royce and with the British Government. By mid-year 1986 the irritation caused by this stream of correspondence was perceived by many observers to be counter-productive. However, despite the antagonism which he was stirring up, Derek retained a strong core of support among Weybridge personnel.

In trying to draw attention to the advantages to British industry and British jobs of a UK-based programme, Derek tried to enlist the support of the Minister responsible for civil aviation matters at the Thatcher government's Department of Trade & Industry, Geoffrey Pattie, but met with disinterest and a feeble dismissal that it was up to British Aerospace to decide the merits of such a programme.

During the course of the year, Derek Lowe tried to construct a plan for the launch and engineering programme for the -500 Series. The re-engining envisaged the use of the Grumman nacelle and thrust reverser (used in the GIV and Fokker 100 aircraft), the expertise of Cranfield College of Aeronautics, which had already prepared a detailed marketing case for the proposal, and the engineering capability of Marshall's of Cambridge and assumed that BAe would collaborate to ensure certification. However, the Rolls-Royce Civil Engine Group, headquartered at Derby, responsible for the Tay programme, had not been approached at all!

Towards the end of the year, Derek decided to convene a meeting and invite all United Kingdom operators known to be interested in One-Eleven re-engining. These included BIA and Dan-Air, who had continued to show their support. Derek was intent on launching a programme particularly based on the -500 Series aircraft and was clearly not aware of Dee Howard's unannounced agreement with BAe to cover that variant as well. The authoritative UK aviation magazine *Flight International* picked up that certain relevant matters had not been made public and revealed the situation in an article on 6 December 1986, entitled *Tay One-Eleven agreements unfurl.* This describes the situation rather well and with the magazine's permission I repeat below some paragraphs from that article.

US company Dee Howard has placed all its cards on the table and revealed that its agreement for re-engining the British Aerospace One-Eleven covers all variants - the -400, -475 and -500 Series.

The announcement comes in the wake of rallying cries for a re-engining programme to give the popular but ageing One-Eleven a new lease of life. Some One-Eleven operators and other interested parties, such as financiers, gathered together recently to discuss the feasibility of replacing the One-Eleven's Spey engines by new Rolls-Royce Tays.

The meeting was called on the assumption that the chief market would be for the One-Eleven 475/500 Series, and not for the corporate Series 400 aircraft which was already the subject of a re-engining programme managed by Dee Howard. It was not known that Dee Howard's agreement also covered the 475 and 500 Series, and several attendees remarked on the noticeable absence of representatives from either British Aerospace or Rolls-Royce, to whom they would have liked to have addressed technical and financial questions.

The Tay One-Eleven could be regarded as a competitor to the British Aerospace 146 or the Tay-powered Fokker 100, which the re-engined One-Eleven would actually outperform. It was therefore assumed that, for political reasons, Rolls-Royce was sitting back and allowing the operators to do the approaching, rather than actively seeking One-Eleven customers.

But one week after the meeting, brought together by Derek Lowe, Director of UK-based Executive Jet Sales, Dee Howard provided the real answer: its agreement, signed almost a year ago with British Aerospace, covers all One-Eleven types. Because of the sensitive marketing issues, the terms of which are still confidential, Dee Howard agreed not to publicise its 475 and 500 Series agreements until a more appropriate time.

While anxious not to upset British Aerospace, the design authority for the One-Eleven, Dee Howard released the following statement to Flight to dispel confusion: "In January 1986 the Dee Howard company and British Aerospace entered into a technical assistance agreement whereby British Aerospace would provide technical assistance to Dee Howard in its programme for the FAA and CAA certified Tay-powered

BAC One-Eleven 400/475/500 aircraft."
British Aerospace confirmed the agreement but stressed that the commercial aspects of it were still confidential. Rolls-Royce also declined to give details of its arrangements with Dee Howard, but pointed out: "We are always willing to discuss any engineering programme with any interested manufacturers and constructors, and we have also talked independently to some One-Eleven operators, including UK airlines". Rolls-Royce said that it did not attend the meeting called by Mr Lowe because, in view of its contractual relationship with British Aerospace and Dee Howard, it felt it would have confused potential customers by attending without its contractual partners.

As noted earlier, the Marshall Company of Cambridge had expressed an interest in the concept of One-Eleven re-engining, considering that work on such a programme would fit in well with Marshall's niche business in aviation. Marshall's expressed an interest to Derek Lowe to undertake the engineering work on the proposal, provided that it had access to all the appropriate BAe design information and provided that it was paid for the work. Marshall's was not prepared to invest speculative money in the programme. These two conditions must have been a stumbling block because Marshall's were not subsequently involved with any of Derek's

Taytime

By Angela Obvious

● How tolerant of time technology can be! Rolls-Royce Tay One-Eleven procrastinations have consumed years, each producing a hundred reasons for not updating Britain's 100-seat jetliner. Now it is fully launched.

BAe is still worried that the Tay One-Eleven might upset the 146 market, and R-R fears that it might upset the Fokker 100. But you can't keep a good engine off a good airframe. If you don't do what the market wants, Dee Howard of Texas will do it anyway.

Fokker and Gulfstream may be upset, but the sky is big enough for all. The Dart-powered 748 was good for the Dart-powered F.27, and for the Gulfstream II, and *vice versa*.

One-Eleven operators—airline and executive—will be delighted to put new whine in ageless bottles, and the Romanians will be very happy to put Tays in new One-Elevens, and revitalise the Bucharest production line.

Let's call it the Tay-Eleven. PS—Those who never take "shut up" for an answer, and have tipped BAe and R-R off their fences, can now advocate something else sensible. How about urging Boeing to go for a 7J7 with underwing turbofans and—possibly the only thing that could worry the Airbus A320—people-pleasing twin aisles?

FLIGHT INTERNATIONAL.

28 February 1987

work on this programme. Also at around this time Marshall's tried to contact the Dee Howard Company to propose that Marshall's could be the European modification centre for Dee Howard customers, but could get nobody in San Antonio to respond.

Derek Lowe's campaign for a UK programme continued into 1987. Note for example a letter to *Flight International,* reproduced with the magazine's permission, in Appendix II. The subject was also highlighted by *Flight International's* humorist Roger Bacon via his fictional correspondent Angela Obvious. (see previous page).

Apart from Derek Lowe there were quite a number of protagonists for a UK-based Tay/One-Eleven re-engining programme, who continued to lament the fact that a US company was undertaking the programme. One of these was the late Ron Wood, formerly Sales Manager of the Civil Aircraft Division of BAe, who retired in the mid-1980s after a distinguished aviation career. In a letter to Derek Lowe, admiring Derek's efforts to try to get a UK programme going, he continues

> *"I, too, tried hard before I left BAe to persuade the BAe Board of the sense of a re-engining development programme. I failed, partly I think, because those responsible for the decision did not recognise at the time the growing attraction to airlines of the development of existing aircraft as opposed to the purchase of 'new/new' equipment and partly because of the recognition that a Tay engined One-Eleven does everything - and more - that a BAe146 can do at half the capital cost. However it is not possible, happily to quash such a good idea, hard as BAe tried and as you know, the Tay re-engining project is being developed by Dee Howard instead of in its natural home, the UK".*

The Dee Howard programme emerges - slowly

In announcing the widening of the Dee Howard programme to include the -475 and -500 Series, it was anticipated that the first flight of the prototype aircraft would be in July 1988 and that aircraft certification would now take place in October 1989. Note that, since programme launch, the projected certification date had slipped from December 1987 to October 1989. This reflects that Dee Howard was beginning to realise the particular problems of the programme that it was now taking on.

Realising that its own aircraft programme was now longer than the engine certification programme for the Tay 650, in early 1987, the Dee Howard Company took the decision to change the engine variant for the production aircraft to the Tay 650, which would be certificated in 1988 for heavier weight Fokker 100 aircraft. This would give all marks of the One-Eleven a better airfield performance and climb performance than the Spey-powered aircraft. However, it was intended that prototype flying would commence with two Tay 610 engines released from the Gulfstream Flight Certification programme. (The Tay 612-14 designation hereafter ceased to exist). It was expected that the Tay 650-14 engine rating for the BAC One-Eleven would be certificated in May 1989.

A development in the funding and management of the programme occurred at the Paris Air Show of June 1987 at which a further agreement was entered into between Mr Dee U Howard and Sheikh Salem Binladen. This agreement valued Sheikh Binladen's contributions towards launching the re-engine programme as $1.5m and gave him a 20% interest in the re-engine programme. Additionally, it was a condition that Dee Howard was not to invest in any other programme until Salem Binladen had been reimbursed his $1.5m. It was also agreed that a separate company was to be set up to own the re-engine programme and its technology, except for the nacelle and thrust reverser.

Marketing the re-engining programme

Towards the latter part of 1987, Rolls-Royce expressed concern for the first time at the lack of visibility of any marketing activity by the Dee Howard Company, to, for example, the several UK operators of the One-Eleven who had earlier shown much interest in re-engining.

Meanwhile, however, continuing discussions between the Dee Howard Company and the Romanians led to the suggestion of Dee Howard getting involved with the certification of Romania's -500 Series aircraft and the supply through Dee Howard of Tay engines for retrofit and new production.

Coincidentally showing interest at this time in the potential of the Tay One-Eleven aircraft was the major aircraft financing and leasing group GPA (originally Guiness Peat Aviation) of Ireland. This interest was particularly in new production (Tay-powered) One-Elevens from Romania. The Dee Howard Company, through Wayne Fagan, was the catalyst for this and tried to construct a consortium to launch a programme. Dee Howard drew into this the Continental Grain Company of the USA, which was active in Romanian counter-trade and which could arrange financing, GPA to purchase and lease out the new aircraft and Dee Howard itself to provide engineering support and procure Tay engines from Rolls-Royce. Dee Howard's had its own goal which was to be reimbursed $13m for its engineering and certification costs. It was hoped that the cost of the new aircraft could be driven down to $16.5m.

The fatal flaw in all of this was the Romanian government/industry structure, with problems of inter-agency politics and the near-impossibility of finding somebody in the Romanian foreign trade organisation or the aircraft factory prepared to declare a price for the construction of the airframes. Remember that this was still the era of the Ceaucescu regime, with paralysis of action and deep suspicions of doing business with the West.

Another interested party was Lovaux, a major One-Eleven aircraft overhaul and maintenance facility which had taken over the production facility vacated by BAe at Hurn, near Bournemouth, England. Lovaux had developed a strong customer base in looking after seven One-Elevens based in Saudi Arabia, several of which were owned by the Saudi National Bank. The operators of these aircraft were all interested in the potential advantages of re-engining.

Overhanging the British end of the support for the Dee Howard programme was the announcement, some time in late 1986, that BAe's Weybridge operations would close by the end of 1988. One-Eleven support was to move to Bristol.

Unfortunately in May 1988 the Dee Howard programme suffered a major setback when the tragic death occurred in a private flying accident of Sheikh Salem Binladen. Ian Munro was subsequently appointed Administrator of the Estate, which succeeded to all the Texas assets of Sheikh Binladen.

CHAPTER THREE

Aeritalia and Swift Aviation

A very significant development for the Tay/One-Eleven, during Spring 1988, was that discussions commenced between the Dee Howard Company and the very large Italian aerospace company, Aeritalia, which was interested in taking a financial stake in the Company, to expand its existing aircraft modification business and gain an industrial foothold in the USA. These discussions led to Aeritalia agreeing to an initial purchase of 40% of Dee Howard's capital.

This was fortuitous for the Dee Howard Company because British Aerospace, Hatfield Division, was raising concerns about the Dee Howard Company's ability to manage and complete the One-Eleven certification programme. There was also concern whether the scope of a Supplemental Type Certificate, which Dee Howard intended to pursue, would be adequate to cover the degree of technical change. Doubts were also raised (again) about the lack of visibility of any marketing by Dee Howard, particularly the submittal of any re-engining offers to the UK BAC One-Eleven operators. For example, the absence of a firm proposal irritated British Island Airways (BIA), which had long been interested in re-engining four One-Eleven aircraft and possibly acquiring additional aircraft. Also irritated was

1988: First installation of a Tay engine on a One-Eleven

Dan-Air, which had 12 -500 Series aircraft and which wished to set itself up to do conversions for other airlines, eg BIA. Dee Howard claimed that the delay was because it was waiting to sign an agreement with Aeritalia. Offer letters to the above two airlines and to Ryan Air and the Ford Motor Company of Europe were not finally released until mid-August.

Meanwhile, in May, two reworked Tay Mk 610 engines, which were fairly similar in configuration to the originally chosen Tay 612s, arrived in San Antonio and a trial installation of one of the engines was made shortly afterwards.

Swift Aviation

A new opportunity to develop a Rolls-Royce Tay-powered BAC One-Eleven aircraft emerged in late 1987, when a small UK leasing company called Swift Aviation, based in Hampshire, proposed to buy up to 25 new Romanian One-Elevens, to be powered by Tay engines, plus 25 options and lease them out to airlines.

Why did Swift Aviation choose the Romanian One-Elevens? Swift had been involved with aircraft leasing but had decided that it wanted to become a principle and own its aircraft, which must be Stage 3 compliant. In pursuing this aim, Managing Director Brian Kyme ran into difficulty with trying to buy new aircraft from Airbus Industrie and noted that most new Boeing aircraft for leasing were going to GPA or ILFC. Chance mention of the Romanian programme by some BAe personnel convinced Kyme that the Tay/One-Eleven was the type of aircraft that could fulfil his ambitions.

The essence of the programme, which developed during 1988, was that Swift Aviation would establish a consortium to buy so-called 'green', ie unpainted, unfitted-out One-Eleven -500 Series airframes from the Romanians, using materials and parts from British Aerospace, supplied through Swift Aviation. The 'green' aircraft would be fitted with Tay engines and Dee Howard nacelles and thrust reversers in Bucharest and then flown to a UK modification or fitting-out centre for completion with interiors, galleys etc. Swift Aviation would then market the new Tay-powered aircraft for leasing.

This arrangement for outside-supplied materials would obviate the need for the Romanians to buy such materials and thus create a Romanian demand for offset or counter-trade. Such offset demands had been a continual headache for the existing Spey/One-Eleven programme. The big advantage of using the Romanian airframe manufacturer was that labour costs in Bucharest were considered to be much less than in the UK.

This was the scheme of things; what was the reaction of the Romanians? Kyme describes his meetings with CNA, the Romanian government's

33

aviation negotiating organisation, as extremely difficult, with little enthusiasm shown and the atmosphere almost hostile. As one might expect from an organisation which was subservient to the communist party machine and ultimately the dictator Ceaucescu, no-one was prepared to make a commitment or decision and Kyme was never allowed to discuss his proposals with anybody at the aircraft factory.

The initial response by BAe, Rolls-Royce and others to this proposal was one of scepticism that Swift Aviation had the credibility and competence to put this programme together. Another concern was that at this time in the Romanian ROMBAC Spey programme, the production rate had only been about one aircraft per year. Some referred to it as a 'cottage industry'. How did Swift Aviation think it was going to improve on this dismal performance?

The Dee Howard Company's position on this proposal was that for any new production application for its nacelle and thrust reverser, the company would want a fee for its design rights of $13m.

Rolls-Royce for its part was also not keen in getting drawn into a consortium with the Romanians, because it might diminish the Company's ability to recover Romanian debts on the existing Licence Agreement.

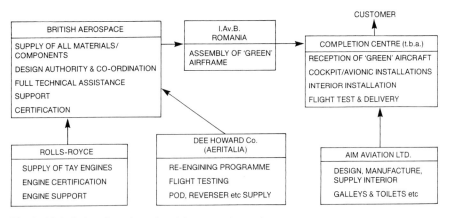

The Swift Aviation (later Associated Aerospace) teaming arrangement

British Aerospace, in its reply to Swift's initial proposal refused to answer some of the questions raised by Swift Aviation about the programme, because of the confidential nature of its contracts with the Romanians and the Dee Howard Company. However, BAe also pointed out the pivotal position it had as Design Authority for the aircraft and that it had to approve any aircraft modifications or changes to its licence agreements. BAe commented that the nature of the programme, which Swift Aviation was proposing, would require expansion of its licence agreement with Romania and the resolution of consequential commercial issues. The proposed teaming arrangements are shown above.

In June, while Swift Aviation was establishing its working arrangements, Rolls-Royce certificated the Tay 650 rating for service in the Fokker 100.

The latter part of 1988 was taken up with Swift Aviation trying to confirm its programme with the Romanians, British Aerospace, Dee Howard and Rolls-Royce, all of which took pains to reserve their positions and existing authority and intellectual property rights. Rolls-Royce, for example, made it quite clear that the sale of engines to Swift Aviation, or through the Dee Howard Company, for the Romanian aircraft should contain no obligations whatsoever for offset or counter-trade in Romania.

Dee Howard - a looming financial crisis

On the other side of the Atlantic and in the closing months of 1988 it was becoming clear that the financial burden on the Dee Howard Company of funding the One-Eleven re-engining programme was becoming no longer bearable. By October $16.5m had been spent on the programme, including $3.5m in technical assistance payments to British Aerospace. Help was now essential and Aeritalia had confirmed its support for the continuance of the programme and agreed to take a further 20% share of the Dee Howard Company, giving it control.

As described in the previous chapter, GPA had shown an interest in buying Tay-powered One-Elevens, considering new production Romanian aircraft in the first instance. When it was found to be impossible for GPA to buy the aircraft at the price which GPA was prepared to pay, GPA's interest switched to re-engined aircraft. Its initial proposal was in having eight BAC One-Eleven -500 Series aircraft re-engined, but GPA was not ready to hurry its decision or place deposits. The eight aircraft were expected to be bought from Philippine Airlines (PAL).

The arrival of this interest from GPA exposed a brittleness in the commercial relationship between Dee Howard and Rolls-Royce, worsened by a somewhat negative or 'hard-ball' attitude by Rolls-Royce. Dee Howard had contracted to purchase eight Tay engines for an initial production run of

-400 Series aircraft, followed by two engines for -500 Series certification. In the light of the possible need for early certification of the -500 Series aircraft for GPA and a slippage anyway in the -400 Series certification programme, Wayne Fagan, acting for Dee Howard sought co-operation in requesting a delay in the delivery of the production engines for the -400 Series. This news was not well received by Rolls-Royce, which claimed to have the production engines already in its engine manufacturing programme. Rather as Wayne Fagan had feared and despite his claims of bad faith, Rolls-Royce started to send invoices for overdue payments and notices that Dee Howard's lack of payments appear *".... as a major item on our company debt"*.

GPA later increased its interest in the programme, writing to Rolls-Royce and asking for a commercial proposal on 22 Tay engines for 11 aircraft, to be valid until the end of January 1989.

At the end of 1988 the Weybridge factory finally closed to all BAe activity.

Marketing developments

Although in the New Year of 1989, Aeritalia had become the majority shareholder of the Dee Howard Company and had brought with it additional capability and financial strength, further delays were apparent in the San Antonio engineering development programme and Rolls-Royce was asked to delay the delivery of the first set of Tay 650 flight certification engines until May. Nevertheless marketing activity was building up and yet another new VP of Marketing was appointed at the Dee Howard Company, the third since the programme started.

Principal prospective customers being pursued at this time were
   -400 Series:
      American Continental
      HM Holdings (a division of the Hanson organisation)
      The Binladen Group
      Ford Motor Company (Europe)
      Turbo-Union
      British Island Airways
   -500 Series:
      Dan-Air
      GPA (considering up to 11 aircraft then owned by Philippine Airlines - PAL)
      TAROM
      Ryan Air (affiliate of GPA)
      Cyprus Airways

36

Programme dates mentioned to these customers were

-400 Series:	First flight:	August 1989
	Certification:	April 1990
-500 Series:	First flight:	April 1990
	Certification:	October 1990

(These changes represented a delay of 34 months since programme launch.)

Of the above prospects confidence was high at Dee Howard of imminently signing up Dan-Air, BIA and GPA. However, GPA was having difficulty in procuring the PAL aircraft. PAL needed the money from selling the One-Eleven's to place as deposits on new Boeing 737-300 aircraft and demanded a price for the One-Elevens which GPA considered very high. Having eventually and reluctantly agreed to this figure, PAL then asked for more and GPA decided to walk out of the negotiations.

To try to draw all these marketing activities together, a major review meeting was hosted by Rolls-Royce on 6 April 1989 at Hatton Cross, London Airport. There were senior representatives from Dee Howard Co, BAe, Dan-Air, BIA, Ryan Air and GPA Group. Nothing seemed to move forward very much and a major opportunity was missed. The operators seemed to be rather concerned about corrosion and life extension on the airframe and the re-financing of the re-engined aircraft. It was still expected that the first flight of the prototype re-engined aircraft would take place at the end of the coming August, but by June the first flight had slipped yet again, this time to December.

The stand-off between GPA and Philippine Airlines on the price of the PAL aircraft resumed in May. GPA intended to set up a re-marketing operation for the re-engined aircraft through an affiliate company, Ryan Air, possibly taking some additional aircraft from British Airways. Of the other customers it was becoming increasingly apparent, however, that while BIA was very keen on re-engining, the airline's financial situation was becoming rather shaky.

Marketing of the -400 Series aircraft to executive operators was intensifying and Rodina Jet Services in the USA were alleged to be negotiating contracts. Turbo-Union, the joint company of Rolls-Royce, MTU and Fiat, which operated a One-Eleven 400 Series aircraft on inter-site communications in Europe was also very interested in the programme.

Swift Aviation's plans develop

Meanwhile, and in parallel with the Dee Howard re-engining programme, Swift Aviation was developing its plans for new-build, Romanian One-Elevens with Tays. In the spring of 1989, Swift Aviation brought in additional management and announced the appointment of Sir Geoffrey Pattie as Chairman. He was a senior Conservative Member of Parliament, who as mentioned earlier had been Minister in charge of the Department of Trade & Industry. He had also been Vice-Chairman of the party's Aviation Committee and Minister of State for Defence Procurement in the early 1980s. Also at about this time the name Associated Aerospace appeared in one or two places though the company's letterhead still firmly referred to Swift Aviation.

A significant problem for Swift Aviation concerned the procuring of a prototype aircraft for development and certification flying. Note that the Swift Aviation programme would use the Romanian -500 Series aircraft, not the -400 Series which was already being prepared for certification by Dee Howard. Romanian airframe number 9, sometimes also referred to as 409, was proposed and would have to be leased or bought from Romania, (provided that they would release it at all), flown to the UK and registered on the UK Register. It would then be flown to San Antonio to join the Dee Howard re-engining certification programme.

Despite its wariness about the complex deal which Swift Aviation was trying to put together, the Chairman of BAe's Civil Aircraft Division, Sydney Gillibrand, wrote to Brian Kyme on 26 September to express BAe's support for the project. The same week Rolls-Royce agreed to negotiate to supply Tay 650 engines to Swift Aviation but, as expected, under certain conditions:

- all payments to be secured and not dependent on the performance of third parties
- no countertrade, compensation trading, or similar
- a firm order for 50 ship sets of engines with options for 50 more
- Rolls-Royce needed to be satisfied with the substance of any third party

Memorandum of Understanding

On 5 July 1989, a Memorandum of Understanding was signed by Associated Aerospace (AAe), alias Swift Aviation, and Tehnoimportexport Foreign Trade Company, which had succeeded the earlier organisation CNA. This MOU confirmed the intention of AAe to purchase from Tehnoimportexport of 50 ROMBAC One-Eleven -500 Series aircraft. This was based on a delivery schedule which called for a first flight of the first production aircraft, referred to as RO11, with Tay engines in August 1991. The MOU recognised that agreements would have to be signed by AAe with BAe and Rolls-Royce for the supply of materials and engines to Tehnoimportexport on a schedule consistent with the proposed Romanian delivery plan.

A difficulty arose in the early autumn of 1989 when AAe tried to secure financing of the project through financial arrangers Babcock & Brown. The latter insisted that financial guarantees should first be signed by Rolls-Royce and BAe, both of whom were still hesitant about the risks involved with such an unknown entity as AAe being able to launch and execute this new programme. Associated Aerospace could not yet guarantee that airline customers would sign up to lease the new aircraft because the programme had not yet been launched.

Rolls-Royce's vacillation (about its for support this programme) continued throughout the autumn and it was not until 30 November that the Company finally made a full price offer to AAe for 50 engines. In addition to attaching conditions to this offer, such as Rolls-Royce not being prepared to enter into any teaming arrangement or partnerships, the Company also wished to be satisfied that the Romanians were fully committed to the project and suggested that AAe should hold a performance bond on the aircraft company with reserved financial funds outside Romania.

Costing the AAe Programme

In its Business Plan, AAe had looked at the unit costs of the programme in terms of two batches, aircraft 1-10, which used parts and materials already held by the Romanians, and aircraft batch 11-50, which involved all-new materials. AAe estimated the cost breakdown for the latter batch as follows, (in millions of US Dollars per aircraft).

1.   Associated Aerospace's cost estimates (per aircraft)

*	BAe materials and components	6.00
*	Dee Howard nacelles and thrust reversers	2.50
*	Romanian labour costs	2.40
*	Avionics	1.00
*	Completion costs	0.20
*	BAe management fees	0.10
*	Warranty and Product Support	0.25
*	Recovery of non-recurring costs	1.00
		13.45

Other Costs:

*	Rolls-Royce Tay engines	4.00
*	Interior kits	0.80
*	Transportation of parts to Romania	0.25
		5.05
	Total	$m 18.50

British Aerospace Commercial Aircraft Ltd, in a letter to AAe in November 1989 about AAe's Business Plan, offered its own estimates and comment on the price of management, support and aircraft parts needed to be supplied to the Romanians for two batches of aircraft, namely 1-10 and 11-50, together with comments on the price of other non-BAe supplies, such as the Tay conversion kits.

Although aircraft 1-10 would be constructed from parts already supplied to Romania for its Spey-powered -500 Series aircraft, BAe pointed out that the inventory was not complete and would require more purchases, worth approximately $31m, to be made to complete the 10 aircraft. Looking at the follow-on batch, aircraft 11-50, we can compare BAe's estimate of the cost of producing the new Romanian aircraft with AAe's estimate.

2. BAe's estimate of the AAe's costs (in millions of US dollars per aircraft)

    *   For materials to be purchased from BAe   5.789

    *   Romanian labour costs for constructing aircraft
        from the AAe-supplied parts   3.000

    *   For the Tay conversion kits purchased by BAe
        from Dee Howard   3.250 - 3.500

    *   The cost to BAe of developing an updated cockpit
        avionics package: estimated to be £39m,spread over
        three years; this could be amortised over 50 aircraft, ie   0.780

    *   Avionics kit price   1.310

    *   Completion centre costs (assuming BAe selected)
        for installation of avionics package, aircraft interior
        kit and long-range fuel tank system and painting of
        completed aircraft   1.659

    *   Warranty and product support costs (BAe)   0.750

    *   BAe management fee   0.100

    Other costs estimated by, but not involving, BAe:

    *   A shipset of Rolls-Royce Tay 650 engines   4.300

    *   Passenger cabin interior and long-range fuel tanks   0.800

    *   Transportation of parts to Romania   0.250
                                                                              ─────────
        Total: Approximately $m 22.000

41

On the basis of BAe's estimates above, the unit cost for the main batch of aircraft (11-50), at about $22m, would be considerably more than the assumption of $18.5m used in Associated Aerospace's Business Plan. This would imply a loss-making programme and overhang AAe's attempts to obtain financing and a programme launch.

Management changes at the Dee Howard Company

Under the influence of the new Aeritalia majority shareholding of 60% in 1989, a new management team was formed in San Antonio, under newly recruited President and CEO Philip Greco and had as Senior Vice Presidents, Wayne Fagan (Commercial Contracts and General Counsel) and Tom Finch (Engineering). An important newcomer was Steve Townes, VP responsible for Plans and Programs and Business Development.

Within two weeks the organisation was changed again! (Frequent management changes were a constant and disturbing feature of the whole Dee Howard programme). The position of Senior Vice President was abolished; Tom Finch was moved aside from line engineering to concentrate on technology development. Wayne Fagan lost the responsibility for commercial contracts and left the company to return to private legal practice. Steve Townes added Sales and Marketing to his responsibility and Dave White came into the company as VP Engineering. A VP post was created for the management of the BAC1-11 programme with Phil Thatch as appointee. Interestingly there was only one senior appointment from Italy in this latest Dee Howard team, the VP for Finance.

Members of the new Dee Howard team visited Rolls-Royce at this time to explain the status of the re-engining programme. It was clearly an embarrassment to Aeritalia and President Greco that the company had repeatedly missed its programme dates and the new urgency was to get the prototype aircraft in the air as quickly as possible and still aim to achieve certification before the end of 1990. It was hinted that the cost of certification might reach $50m. It was also admitted that marketing had been feeble and still no contracts had been signed. (Marketing activity had not been helped by the call from Greco for a halt in the production of new sales brochures and publicity material on the One-Eleven programme while he assessed the state of the programme).

In September, GPA emerged again with a statement claiming that they now held title to the 10 PAL BAC One-Eleven -500s and requested a fresh proposal from the Dee Howard Company increased to 13 firm plus 37 options for re-engining. GPA tried to negotiate for a re-engining price of $3m per aircraft (not including the engines). The discount implied by this was not acceptable to Dee Howard and methods were sought to limit any price discounts to only the 'firm' aircraft.

Increasing pressure on the Dee Howard programme

In view of the continuing slippage of the flight programme, the Dee Howard Company started looking for another -400 Series aircraft, to try to reduce the time needed to achieve the required programme of flight certification tests. BAe continued outwardly to express its support for the programme and supply of data for certification purposes; it was rumoured that the Technical Assistance Agreement was extremely favourable to BAe and costly to the Dee Howard Company.

The problems of trying to certify the programme quickly and secure orders and deposits to alleviate the cash flow imbalance were exemplified by the qualified interest by two new potential customers, Turbo-Union and the Coastal Corporation, both of which were showing interest in having their aircraft re-engined but wished to see the Dee Howard prototype make its first flight before ordering. This caution was in due course expressed by other potential customers and represented a serious 'Catch 22' situation for the Dee Howard Company.

The Dee Howard aircraft being modified for re-engining

Into October 1989 the major structural changes to the fuselage at the engine mount plane were complete. However, shortage of parts, for example the final standard of crane beams, from which the engine is suspended, continued to be a major problem.

I suggested earlier that Rolls-Royce management appeared not to give support for the Dee Howard programme with the same enthusiasm as for the Fokker 100 and Gulfstream IV programmes. This is reflected in the provision of engineering representation at the Dee Howard facility. In fact, it was not until the beginning of 1989 that a Rolls-Royce engineer (John Charlton, reporting to Jack Mullins at Rolls-Royce's Atlanta office) was seconded to San Antonio. Even then his job was split between the Tay/One-Eleven and supporting Dee Howard Engineering in making proposals for re-engining the DC9 and other aircraft with a further development of the Tay, known as the Tay 670. When these latter studies faltered, in late 1989, John Charlton was withdrawn, leaving the Dee Howard programme without support for a period until early 1990, when Malcolm Sellar became resident and Jon Taylor started visiting to attend the flight test programme.

There was a press announcement that the first flight of the first re-engined aircraft was now expected to be on 12 February 1990. Whether or not it was because the delay to the first flight might in reality be even worse than announced, Phil Thatch, VP of Program Management, resigned on 2 November, only three months after being appointed.

On the marketing side, all attention was becoming focused on the necessity of a sizeable programme launch and the prospect of GPA launching with an order which was now for 15 firm plus 35 option -500 Series aircraft. However, the continual slippage and delays in the programme were causing GPA considerable unease. R&D costs were believed to have risen to $60m. Another concern was that the -500 Series aircraft (with Spey engines) had never been certificated in the USA. Would certificating a major change to an aircraft, which did not have a Federal Aviation Administration Certificate already, prove to be an insuperable task? GPA appointed a consultant to advise them on this.

The importance attached to a GPA launch, which would clearly establish the credibility of the re-engine programme is indicated by the holding of a Chairman-level meeting between Aeritalia and GPA (but without any Dee Howard personnel present) in London in October 1989. The meeting went well and Aeritalia signalled a strong desire to certificate the -500 series aircraft. A Memorandum of Understanding was signed by the Chairmen in December for 15 firm and 35 option conversions. Notwithstanding this agreement, there were many in GPA and its daughter company, Ryan Air, who had little confidence that the Dee Howard Company would certificate the -500 Series by mid 1991.

CHAPTER FOUR

1990: an eventful year

At the end of 1989, a further Memorandum of Understanding, (MOU) was signed between Associated Aerospace (Aae) and BAe (Commercial Aircraft) Ltd, recording the intention of the parties to enter into contractual negotiations associated with the purchase of 50 new production ROMBAC 2560 aircraft (as the Romanian-built, Tay-powered aircraft was to be called). The MOU confirmed arrangements for Aae to purchase aircraft materials from BAe and for BAe to procure conversion kits for the Tay installation from Dee Howard, including design information. BAe was also committed to negotiating terms for the development of an avionics package, for the modernisation of the One-Eleven's cockpit and would negotiate an agreement for BAe to complete some of the partly finished aircraft at one of its facilities.

Notwithstanding Aae's intention to manage the programme and to supply to IAvB, Romania all the aircraft materials (except engines), which had been procured and stored for Aae by BAe, it was agreed that BAe would undertake the management of Aae's interests in Romania, but would not assume responsibilities for Romanian performance. BAe would also negotiate with Dee Howard about the use of a Romanian aircraft for certification flying and for the undertaking by Dee Howard to obtain FAA and CAA certification of the conversion kit.

On 8 February 1990, Rolls-Royce signed a MOU with Associated Aerospace on a similar basis to that signed by BAe and covering the sale of engines. The MOU called for first Tay engine deliveries six months before aircraft deliveries, which in turn were quoted as 2-4 aircraft in 1991, 6-8 aircraft in 1992 and thence 10 aircraft per year thereafter. (Note that since the start of Romania's production of Spey-powered aircraft, the aircraft factory had only managed to deliver about ONE aircraft per year!).

GPA withdraws

The prospects for a successful BAC One-Eleven/Tay re-engining programme suffered a major setback at the beginning of February 1990 when the Board of GPA decided that it could no longer support the programme. It was reported by a GPA senior to a Rolls-Royce colleague that GPA *"viewed the risks far outweighed the benefits, particularly with their view of a projected glut of new aircraft in 1992/93"*. GPA claimed that it was not against the concept of One-Eleven re-engining but decided that it didn't suit the company's leasing portfolio. Note that GPA was intending to lease the re-engined One-Elevens into the same market into which Associated Aerospace was intending to place its new (Tay-powered) One-Eleven aircraft.

The significance of GPA's withdrawal was possibly overlooked at the time when there was so much pre-occupation with getting the prototype -400 aircraft into the air. However, GPA would have provided the impetus of a large launch order from a very credible customer. Another smaller setback occurred at this time when previously interested British Island Airways asked for its shares to be suspended on the Unlisted Securities Market. BIA blamed a severely depressed market for package holidays in the Mediterranean.

Despite these setbacks Aeritalia was determined to continue with the programme with a view to trying to recoup the $65m which had already been invested. Note the continuing build-up in development costs.

In departing the scene GPA allegedly indicated that it would be willing to make available one of the ex-Philippine One-Eleven aircraft, if some other company wanted to launch a programme. However, Philippine Airlines (PAL) was adamant that the BAC One-Elevens were still theirs and nothing had ever been signed with GPA. PAL was even interested in having five of their aircraft re-engined on their own behalf. However, PAL's enthusiasm was blunted by repeated unsuccessful attempts to start a dialogue with the Dee Howard Company.

Helijet

Hardly had the matter of GPA's withdrawal from the One-Eleven re-engine programme died down when there was a sudden flurry of interest in the programme by a company called Helijet. Little was known about the company except that it had been formed by an Australian entrepreneur and had its registered office in the Australian outback, together with a small office in Dallas, Texas. A 60% majority ownership in the company was held by a Japanese investment organisation, EIE. Such was Helijet's apparent enthusiasm for the re-engine programme that it persuaded Roger Munt, then recently appointed VP of Sales and Marketing of the Dee Howard Company, to leave his position there to take charge of negotiations on behalf of Helijet (US) Inc.

Helijet tried to persuade EIE to invest in a programme to re-engine 12 firm and 38 option One-Eleven -500 Series aircraft, which would be purchased from the world-wide market. This was at a time when the Dee Howard Company was still struggling to get the prototype -400 Series aircraft flying and had still not made a formal commitment to launch the -500 Series re-engining, although that was clearly their intention. The pursuit of this business was characterised by poor communications, cautiousness about the credibility of Helijet and the commitment of EIE. After a couple of months of the various personnel trying to come together to discuss a deal, EIE withdrew its support and Helijet was obliged to try to seek financial support from other Japanese banks. Eventually nothing came of this and Helijet faded from view.

The Jaffe Group and Romania

While Helijet was occupying Dee Howard's attention, two alternative developments were emerging in Romania. The first involved a visit to Bucharest by Texas entrepreneur Douglas Jaffe, who owned an aircraft modification business called Comtran at San Antonio airport, which specialised in upgrading used Boeing 707 aircraft. The purpose of Jaffe's visit was to deliver engine hush kits for the B707 formerly owned by President Ceaucescu and receive in barter four unused JT3D engines which Jaffe required for another customer of Comtran. The visit was one of the first by an American trading company since Ceaucescu's execution and was received with great enthusiasm, a matter which was reported in very colourful terms by the magazine *Texas Monthly*.

While in Bucharest, Jaffe toured the Romanian Aircraft Factory and decided that if the ROMBAC One-Eleven could be modified to include new engines, it could be marketed around the world as both a freighter and passenger airliner. Just before he left, Jaffe signed a MOU with Eugeniu Smirnov, Managing Director of the aircraft factory, for the factory to increase production of One-Elevens to 8-10 per year. *Texas Monthly*, in its article, makes no mention of the Dee Howard Company, nor the prototype re-engined aircraft which was about to fly, nor of who was going to supply the new engines which were talked about. Nothing more seems to have been heard about Jaffe's One-Eleven proposals but one result of the Bucharest visit was the setting-up of a joint trading company called JARO (short for Jaffe-Romanian), which would handle all Jaffe's deals in Romania. JARO continues in business and remains the principal legacy of Jaffe's much lauded visit.

Hush kits

A potentially more serious distraction from Associated Aerospace's programme for new production of Tay-powered One-Elevens emerged in May, when the Minister of Machine Building, Andrei Pintilie, persuaded a visiting Rolls-Royce team headed by Dr David Mitchell to hear a presentation on a Spey hush kit proposal by Professor Buriana, who was

Managing Director of the Romanian Engine Factory, ITmB. The hush kit consisted of sound absorbent liners in the engine intake and an ejector silencer mounted on the back of the engine.

In parallel with the enthusiasm for hush kits by Minister Pintilie, it was announced in June that A J Walter, a UK aircraft trading and leasing company specialising in BAC One-Eleven aircraft, had signed a contract with ROMBAC to become the world-wide agent for the sale and leasing of all Romanian-built aircraft. As part of the agreement, A J Walter would work with the Quiet Nacelle Corporation to offer a Stage 3 hush-kitted version of the Spey-powered ROMBAC 475 and 500 Series One-Elevens.

Whether the proposed QNC hush kit embodied any of the concepts shown by Professor Buriana a few months previously is not known. It is sobering to note that a hush kit for the One-Eleven, capable of achieving Stage 3 compliance for the -400 Series, was not certificated until ten years later.

It is interesting to note that the Managing Director of A J Walter, in announcing his deal, did not ignore the Associated Aerospace programme for new production Tay-powered One-Elevens and felt that there was enough room in the market for both programmes. Once again, observers expressed doubts as to whether Romanian industry could sustain a production of as many as 13 aircraft a year by 1995, as suggested by A J Walter.

Towards an Associated Aerospace launch

Associated Aerospace had been watching warily the sudden enthusiasm for hush kits generated by Minister Pintilie but had decided to ignore this diversion and press on with its own programme, which was getting close to its official launch. As it turned out, at a time of great upheaval in Romanian governance, the hush kit programme did not survive the initial discussion phase.

During this period, an unexpectedly critical, some might even say mischievous, letter was received by AAe's Chairman, Sir Geoffrey Pattie, from Derek Lowe, who had previously been such an enthusiastic supporter of re-engining. One of the letter's themes was that the programme was too late in starting and that the market window of opportunity had all but closed. Another criticism was the limitation of the Tay's turbo-annular combustion system and what Lowe alleged were inferior emissions characteristics. AAe asked for Rolls-Royce's comments on this and the Company retorted that Tay emissions levels were far below both existing regulations and also below those levels which one might expect to become the next stage in the process of lower emissions regulations.

Further progress was made by AAe on 29 June 1990 when it signed a

48

Purchase Contract with the Romanian Aircraft Factory, IAvB, for the purchase of 50 One-Eleven aircraft.

The Associated Aerospace Tay/One-Eleven programme was officially launched on 30 July when the contract for the 50 aircraft with IAvB was announced. (This was nearly a month after the first flight of the Dee Howard prototype conversion, a description of which is covered in the next chapter). It was expected then that the first delivery of a 'green' aircraft from Romania would take place before the end of 1991. The overall value of the programme was given as $1 billion.

The management team was formally announced as Sir Geoffrey Pattie (Chairman), Brian Kyme (Managing Director), Chris Hamshaw-Thomas (Marketing Director), John Farrand (Contracts Director) and with Brian Trubshaw and John Rogers as Consultants to the Board.

Rolls-Royce also signed a contract on this day for the supply of Tay 650 engines but it was a contract which was only activated when certain conditions were fulfilled, in particular the payment of deposits on the engines.

Impression of the proposed AAe One-Eleven

A comprehensive report on AAe's launch appeared in the American journal *Aviation Week and Space Technology* on 6 August and it was reported additionally that equity funding for the programme of the order of $60m had been organised through Belmont London, a subsidiary of Banque Financiere Parisienne. (This source had not previously been mentioned). All other agreements were claimed to be in place. No mention was made of which UK centre would complete the aircraft after the 'green' airframes had been flown in from Romania.

Concern about market prospects

Back in San Antonio with the Dee Howard Company, the sales position of the re-engining programme looked rather bleak. With GPA gone, hopes for a Helijet order fading away and no visibility of any other major One-Eleven re-engine orders in the offing, Aeritalia as owner of Dee Howard was once again alarmed about the deteriorating financial position of the programme - large sums were being spent on trying to achieve the first flight but no money was coming in from orders or deposits. Accordingly Aeritalia management in Rome appointed Anders Folkedal, an experienced aerospace marketeer from California to review Dee Howard's marketing activity and try to get it going again, with some fresh ideas.

Folkedal was alarmed at what he found. Supposed deals with corporate operators of the -400 Series aircraft did not exist and some potential customers had been ignored. A review of the prospects for business with the 22 -400 Series aircraft in corporate operation revealed the following:

Contract signed (HM Industries)   1
Contract discussions in progress   4
Contact with customer ongoing   3
Withdrawal of interest   1

No apparent recent contact   13

Anders Folkedal immediately tried to kick-start some life into the marketing process and draw upon his wide contacts and experience in the US aircraft business.

During this period in Spring 1990, another event took place which was to have a significant effect later on the BAC One-Eleven programme. This was the acceptance by United Parcel Service of proposals by Aeritalia and Rolls-Royce for the re-engining of 40 firm plus 40 option, Boeing 727-100 aircraft, each with three Tay 651 engines. This variant of the Tay family was very similar in configuration to the Tay 650 of the BAC One-Eleven and Fokker 100 but with a significant increase in climb thrust. The new installation would use essentially the same powerplant (nacelle and thrust reverser) as the One-Eleven.

Yet another proposal - NewBAC

Towards the end of June, just before the first flight, there was ever growing concern about the marketing position. A Rolls-Royce team headed by Charles Cuddington (Head of Marketing) was invited to Rome for a meeting with Aeritalia top management. It emerged that the BAC One-Eleven re-engining programme was top of corporate Aeritalia's 'worry list'. Aeritalia foresaw that re-engining of the -400 Series would only sell at a slow rate to corporate customers and that Aeritalia needed a significant order for -500 Series aircraft to be re-engined, in order to recover its massive R & D costs.

Aeritalia considered that the British Airways (BA) fleet of 34 aircraft was the key to the problem but since BA had expressed no interest in re-engining these aircraft, the answer was to place an option-to-purchase with BA, have the aircraft re-engined and then put them on the market. In looking for potential customers a leasing company would be preferred, or an airline or group of airlines.

It was recognised that Aeritalia and Rolls-Royce might have to take some financial share in this investment if the third party was not able to shoulder the whole cost. Aeritalia went away to work up this proposal, the concept being given the provisional name, NewBAC.

Preparation for first flight

In the hectic build-up to the first flight of the prototype re-engined aircraft relationships between the Dee Howard Company and British Aerospace were becoming strained. An example of this was the matter of ground vibration testing. This is a test where the aircraft is shaken on the ground to establish whether there are any dangerous resonances which might become a hazard in flight. Sometime previously this testing had been programmed for late May (1990) and now, notwithstanding that the aircraft was about to fly, BAe insisted that Dee Howard Co hold up the flight programme so that BAe could prepare the aircraft and install vibration monitoring equipment. BAe had a programme of use for this equipment on several different aircraft programmes and claimed that if the equipment was not used now it would not be available again until the end of the year.

First installed engine ground runs were conducted in early May, in a shade temperature of 36 degrees Celsius. There were a number of problem reports

The Dee Howard Tay/One-Eleven shortly before its first flight

or 'squawks' for high temperatures inside the engine cowlings. The cowling design was very tight over the engine and ventilation airflow was inadequate.

Eventually after taxi runs and other tests, the paperwork for the first flight was cleared on Sunday 1 July 1990, but thunderstorms in the San Antonio area prevented flight that day.

CHAPTER FIVE

First flight and engineering retrospect

The first flight of a Tay-powered BAC One-Eleven, the Dee Howard owned -400 series aircraft, finally took place on Monday 2 July 1990 at 9.50am Central Time from San Antonio International Airport, Texas. The flight lasted 1 hour and 47 minutes and a fine picture of the aircraft is shown on the front cover. The BAe pilot gave a favourable report on the aircraft and its engines and mentioned only two 'squawks', pylon overheating and wing leading edge fuel leaks.

The astonishing sequel was that an immediate senior-level communication was received from Aeritalia headquarters in Rome, by British Aerospace and Rolls-Royce, that there was to be no local or supplier-generated publicity for the first flight and that an announcement would be delayed for a few days while Aeritalia decided how it was going to release the details! After all the programme delays this publicity black-out was hard to comprehend. Nobody at the Dee Howard Company could understand the logic behind the silence and Dee Howard's Public Relations Manager left the company at short notice shortly after this debacle.

Why was the first flight so delayed?

It will be recalled that when the Dee Howard programme was launched in January 1986 it was projected that the first flight of a prototype re-engined aircraft would take place in July 1987. The first flight actually took place exactly three years later in July 1990. What went wrong? Why was it three years later than expected?

This delay had a serious impact on customer confidence that re-engining was something in which they should invest. Just after the first flight, one of the Rolls-Royce engineering representatives on site was asked by Rolls-Royce management to write his comments on the conduct of the programme (from an engineering point of view). His comments were frank and highlighted four problems as he saw them:

1. the Dee Howard Company's unfamiliarity with a programme of this complexity and size

2. the uneven interaction between the parties involved (Dee Howard originals, British Aerospace, Aeritalia secondees)

3.   the Dee Howard policy of hiring and firing workers and management *"with a frequency unusual even for an American company"*

4.   the poor maintenance state of the flight test aircraft.

To these the author would add, from his own personal observation, three more:

*   inadequate programme management,

*   a misjudgement of the cost of the programme and an insufficient and unsteady stream of programme financing

*   an enthusiasm, particularly in the period 1988-90 for trying to launch additional re-engining programmes, such as the DC9 and Boeing 737, which diluted engineering manpower and took management's mind off the speedy prosecution of the One-Eleven programme.

Looking at the four points of the representative's analysis, his comment about Dee Howard's unfamiliarity with a complex programme like this is not a universally held view. Few question the engineering skills of Tom Finch and his team and point for example to the company's success in designing and installing a three-storey elevator into the forward section of a Head of State's Boeing 747. Even Boeing were alleged to be impressed by this. In this chapter we will look at the engineering aspects of Dee Howard's programme.

There certainly appear to have been difficulties in harnessing together the three aircraft teams - BAe (the design authority), the resident Dee Howard personnel and the Italian personnel brought over to Texas for the BAC programme. Many felt that BAe was only supporting the programme under sufferance and because of its contractual commitment. Another Rolls-Royce engineer attached to the programme remarked that when BAe personnel were asked by Dee Howard to provide data to aid certification, they would only do so if specifically contracted to supply those items and they would never hurry over the supply. To give another example, when Dee Howard requested the secondment of a BAe maintenance engineer, there was extended haggling as to how much Dee Howard would pay for his hotel and subsistence before he would be allowed to come. Some claim that there was also a residue of resentment among the Texans about Aeritalia's take-over of Dee Howard.

Previous passages in this narrative have already mentioned the frequent changes of Dee Howard personnel. (Rolls-Royce is not immune from this criticism; in the 11-year period of interest in the Tay/BAC One-Eleven the Company had eight different Managers of the Tay Project - variously called Project Director or Head of Project). Another unsettling factor in Dee Howard Engineering was that a number of engineers were stopped and re-started on the programme as many as four times. This was a point picked up by the magazine *Flight International* in an article on 27 March 1991.

The maintenance state of the flight test aircraft was highlighted on several occasions in status reports from Rolls-Royce representatives in San Antonio. Even before the first flight, Dee Howard engineering had found it necessary to remove and refit the whole tailplane assembly.

Tay/One-Eleven: the engineering changes

Let's now look at the Tay engine installation and what changes the Dee Howard engineers made to the One-Eleven to accommodate the Tay engine in place of the existing the Spey engine.

Engine mounting

The Rolls-Royce Tay engine was illustrated briefly in Chapter One and a larger cutaway drawing is attached, facing page 58.

The two-shaft engine has a front fan diameter - the 'characteristic' dimension - of 45 inches (114.3 cm). The engine has three mounting points. The front mounting consists of a bolted attachment point on a flange of the intermediate casing, which is a major structural casing towards the front of the engine. The mounting point is just outboard of top dead centre. Also on this same intermediate casing is a circular trunnion attachment adjacent to the aircraft pylon or stub wing. The trunnion is located slightly below the engine's horizontal centre line. The third engine mounting is a bolted attachment to a flange on the turbine rear casing. This is at top dead centre.

The engine is suspended at the front and rear casing locations from two steel mounting beams, commonly referred to as 'crane beams', which are Dee Howard-designed aircraft parts and which are bolted to the aircraft's stub wing as illustrated overleaf.

The front beam carries the engine by means of a short connecting link to the flange. The rear crane beam carries the rear of the engine on a pair of short suspension links. The forward trunnion carries thrust loads into the engine pylon. To prevent forward or reverse thrust loads deforming the pylon there is a thrust strut running from the trunnion mounting to a thrust reaction member which is attached to the aircraft side fuselage.

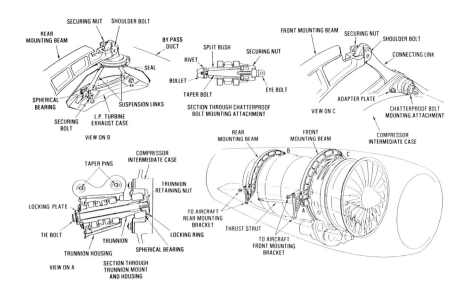

Illustration of Tay engine mounts

Engine mock-up with crane beams and thrust strut in foreground

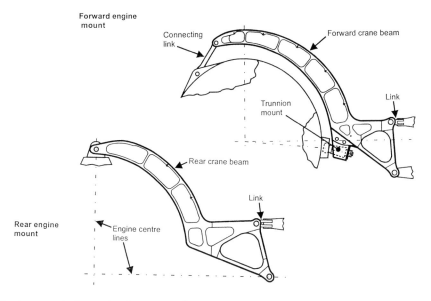

Forward engine mount

Connecting link

Forward crane beam

Trunnion mount

Link

Rear crane beam

Link

Rear engine mount

Engine centre lines

Engine mounts: forward and rear crane beams

This crane beam type of engine mounting is unusual in twin jet aircraft. The civil Spey engine had a similar type of arrangement although, of course, for a smaller diameter engine. Other marks of the Tay engine have crane beams but of slightly different configuration to suit the other aircraft applications. The well known Pratt & Whitney JT8D engine, on the other hand, has a totally different arrangement in which the engine is supported at the front from a wishbone-shaped piece attaching only at the side of the engine and a similar side mounting at the rear

Thrust reverser

During the launch of the Tay programme, Rolls-Royce considered at length whether it had the resources to design and engineer the powerplant for the Tay alongside all the other commitments that it had. The Company decided against undertaking the powerplant, with the result that the Gulfstream IV and Fokker 100 powerplants were designed by Grumman (whose original executive jet business was taken over by Gulfstream Aerospace). For various reasons, not least because the Grumman thrust reverser was

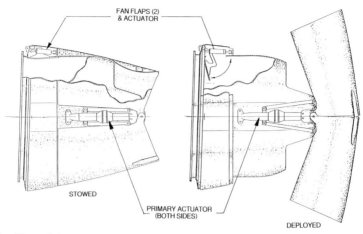

FAN FLAPS (2)
& ACTUATOR

STOWED

PRIMARY ACTUATOR
(BOTH SIDES)

DEPLOYED

The Dee Howard thrust reverser

perceived to be rather heavy, the Dee Howard Company proposed instead to employ on the One-Eleven a totally different design of thrust reverser which it had developed very successfully for a number of business jet aircraft, including the HS125 and Lear Jet. The concept had originally been developed by Etienne Fage, of the French company Astech, from whom Dee Howard had bought the rights. The Dee Howard reverser is very light and has single operating links of each side and a unique feature of flaps in the jet pipe ducting which mix the cool bypass air with the hot core stream and allow the reverser casing to run very cool. This casing is constructed of aluminium alloy.

Cowlings

The Dee Howard Company designed its own cowlings for the One-Eleven conversion. The main components are the cylindrical nose cowl, two cowling doors - which hinge upwards and downwards respectively to expose the engine casings for maintenance purposes - and a fixed cowl which envelopes the crane beam attach points. The location of this cowl means that it has to be in place before the engine is installed. Rearward of the opening cowl doors is another, cylindrical, rear-fixed cowl and then follows the thrust reverser. An external view of the aircraft's cowling is shown below.

58

Rear of the Dee Howard aircraft, showing the engine cowlings

The aircraft installation

The attached foldout illustration shows a cutaway of the Tay-powered One-Eleven as developed by the Dee Howard Company and is reproduced here by kind permission of *Flight International*, in whose journal it was originally published.

Aircraft changes

The changes to the airframe stem from the need for the aircraft to absorb the higher thrust and greater weight of the Tay 650 engine. Because the Tay and Spey engines have essentially the same length of high pressure system, it was possible to design the forward and rear crane beam positions to be the same longitudinal distance apart (56.25 inches). This enabled the crane beam attach points to be located on the same aircraft frames as the Spey-powered aircraft. This means that aircraft strengthening has been concentrated on reinforcing the existing frames, adding appropriate stiffeners and replacement of stringers by redesigned stronger components. New stronger pylons were designed to accommodate the new crane beams and the larger bending moment caused by the Tay being heavier and having its centre of gravity further outboard from the aircraft.

Systems and other changes

While the points on the engine where air is tapped off for cabin air-conditioning have not been changed between the Tay and the Spey, the air on the Tay is at a higher temperature and pressure, due to the higher engine overall pressure. Accordingly a redesigned air-cooler had to be installed in the stub wing. The Spey-powered aircraft generated its electrical supply and was started by a Constant Speed Drive Unit and Starter, which was not too reliable. The Tay engine was designed from the outset with an Integrated Drive Generator and AiResearch starter and this was also incorporated into Dee Howard's One-Eleven. There was also a small change to the gear train in the engine's external gearbox to accommodate an additional hydraulic pump for the aircraft hydraulics.

Weights

Although the basic engine weight difference between a Spey 511 or 512 and the Tay 650 is about 800 lb, this weight difference multiplies when you add in the extra weight of the larger powerplant (cowling, reversers etc) and the weight of the aircraft strengthening. The weight of the Tay installation gradually increased during the development phase and I have tried to resolve the different estimates in the following paragraph, using as a datum the only full breakdown available to me, which is from a Dee Howard weight status report of November 1989.

Compared with a -400 Series aircraft with the Spey 511-14 engines with, or without, Stage 2 hush kits, the Tay 650-powered aircraft was projected by Dee Howard to be 2794 lb, or 3090 lb heavier respectively. For the larger -500 Series aircraft a similar comparison is not available but we can estimate the difference by noting that the difference in total installed weight of two hush-kitted Spey 512-14DW engines relative to Spey 511s is 540 lb, quite a lot of the extra weight being due to the demineralised water system associated with the DW rating. Thus on the -500 Series aircraft the additional weight for re-engining with Tays was expected to be about 2250 lb. On the last published performance estimate (referred to below), a weight difference of 3200 lb was used. Possibly, though not stated, the additional 950 lb was added to allow for the ballast being required in the aircraft's nose in order to restore balance.

Aircraft performance

The excellent performance improvement that would come from substituting Tays for Speys was highlighted in the first BAe brochures of 1983. For example, on the -400 Series in executive configuration, a range improvement of about 18% was projected.

Some refinement of the numbers took place when the Dee Howard Company became responsible for estimating the performance of the aircraft and detailed design and weight estimations had taken place. The range and fuel burn performance published in mid-1989, and which I tabulate below, was not subsequently altered, even after test flying had taken place. One reason for this is that the Dee Howard flight test programme omitted to include any specific air range or back-to-back Spey/Tay flight comparisons. Rolls-Royce pressed Dee Howard to include some extra flights for performance testing, to try to substantiate the published estimates, but the state of the flight programme at the time was such that this request was ignored.

Four possible applications were evaluated at the time, the shorter body -400 Series in executive and airline configuration and the -500 Series with the same two configurations. The two most marketed at the time were the -400 as an executive or corporate aircraft and the -500 in airline configuration and I will confine myself to these.

BAC One-Eleven-400 series, in executive configuration; performance comparison with 33,000 lb fuel

	Spey 511-14	Tay 650
Max take-off weight (lb)	88,500	91,500
Payload (lb)	1,820	1,820
Range at Long Range Cruise* (at ISA+10) (nautical miles)	2,615	3,050 (+17%)
Balance field length at sea level (feet)		
ISA day	8,150	6,600 (-19%)
ISA + 20 day	10,700	7,300 (-32%)

*Assumes 4,500 lb reserve fuel; 150 nm diversion with 30 mins hold

BAC One-Eleven-500 series, airline configuration; performance comparison with 24,860 lb fuel

	Spey 512-14DW	Tay 650
Max take-off weight (lb)	104,500	104,500
Basic Operating Weight (lb)	56,632	59,832
Payload of 109 pasengers (lb) (at 195lb per person)	21,320	21,320
Range at Long Range Cruise (at ISA+10°C) (nautical miles)	1,360	1,523 (+12%)
Balance field length at sea level (feet)		
ISA day	9,020	7,400 (-18%)
ISA + 20° day	Not possible at this weight	8,100

Reserves assumptions similar to the -400

In executive configuration, the Tay-powered -500 Series aircraft with a maximum tankage of 40,000 lb and a maximum take-off weight of 104,500 lb would have a range of approximately 3,500 nautical miles. This would give a comfortable transatlantic, London-New York capability and this advantage in range over the -400 Series aircraft is what led Derek Lowe to consider that a -500 Series re-engine programme had more potential than the -400 chosen as the starting point of the Dee Howard programme.

In addition to the performance gains summarised above, there was also expected to be a significant improvement in climb performance from the more powerful Tay engines but there seems to have been little attempt to quantify the gain.

The Tay/One-Eleven and its competitors

What about the competition to the Tay-powered BAC One-Eleven? In the early days of the re-engining programme with the Dee Howard Company, there really wasn't a competition at all. The programme was targeted at the 20 to 30 One-Eleven -400 Series aircraft which were already owned and operated for VIP, Corporate and Executive duties mostly in the USA. The business decision for the owners of these aircraft was either to re-engine with Tays, perhaps for noise or increased range capability reasons, or not to bother.

It was only with the advent of the Associated Aerospace programme to launch new production Tay-powered One-Elevens, and the campaigns with the European charter airlines and with GPA, that competition with other aircraft types became an issue. AAe saw the main competition for its One-Elevens to be the BAe 146-300 and the Fokker 100 and rather dismissed these as specialised aircraft with much inferior range. The charts below, taken from an AAe sales brochure, illustrate the competitive situation for a number of then current 100-seat aircraft.

Little or no comment was attached to the charts, for example to explain away the Tay/One-Eleven's fuel burn disadvantage compared with the Fokker 100. It will be recalled that no performance measurements were taken on Dee Howard's -400 Series aircraft and hence there was no validation of the estimates which could be read across to the AAe -500 Series aircraft.

The Fokker 100, being an aircraft designed 20 years later than the BAC One-Eleven, had the advantage of 20 years general development in aerospace technologies. By virtue of having a shorter range and less structure and weight to carry fuel, the Fokker 100 was expected to have about 7% lower fuel consumption per seat than the Tay-powered One-Eleven, (based on the latter's brochure performance, estimated by BAe and Dee Howard).

AAe's operating cost comparison suggests a virtual parity between the two aircraft. The key parameter on which AAe was hoping to capitalise was first cost and as noted earlier, even here there were question marks about AAe's estimates for the One-Eleven and its guesses of the 'costs' of the competition.

Notes on the economic case for re-engining

It is not the intention to use this little historical monograph to champion the economic case for re-engining. Many sceptics are doubtful if there ever is a case. The high capital cost of re-engining has to be balanced by the savings produced and these are principally fuel-burn saving and reduction in engine maintenance costs. From the author's experience the numbers won't begin to work unless the fuel saving is at least 10-12%, relative to before re-engining. On the BAC One-Eleven it was predicted to be 15-17%. On the very successful Cammacorp DC8 re-engine programme the saving was about 25%.

As regards engine maintenance costs, the saving in dollars per hour on a mature Tay 650 engine relative to a mature Spey 512-14DW engine was

RANGE

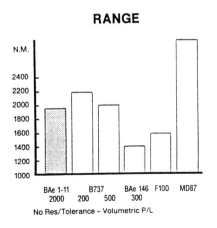

FUEL COSTS

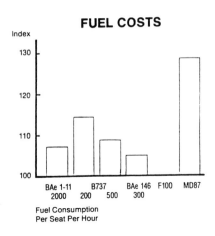

STANDING CHARGES^x

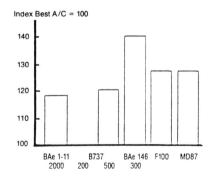

INDICATIVE/COMPARATIVE OPERATING COSTS – PER SEAT MILE

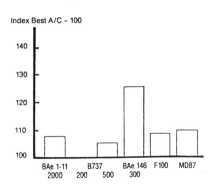

The Tay/One-Eleven and its competitors - AAe's comparisons

64

expected to be 50%. Furthermore, when a new engine commences operation it should have several years in its early life when little maintenance is required and few spare parts consumed. This is the so-called 'honeymoon period' and the savings could be worth up to $1.5m per aircraft.

Because this honeymoon period takes place over a period of time, the conventional method of making aircraft comparisons - by direct operating costs - is not appropriate, because direct operating costs are compared at a given instant in time. With re-engining it is much more appropriate to conduct a net present value (NPV) analysis where the fuel and maintenance savings are represented as a stream of cash flows over, say, 10 years. These cash flows are discounted back to the present day. This was the technique used by United Parcel Service in 1990 in evaluating the case for re-engining its fleet of Boeing 727-100 freighter aircraft with Tay 651 engines. UPS found that re-engining would give a positive NPV and this was a factor in UPS launching that programme.

There are some other benefits which need to be considered in the NPV calculation, such as any revenue raised by the sale of the discarded engines (Speys in this case) and the advantage of not having to buy hush kits (if available and if they guaranteed legislation compliance) to deal with the aircraft noise problem. Additionally the re-engined aircraft with its longer range offers the potential of new routes and additional payload revenue increments.

The author is not aware of an NPV Analysis being carried out on the re-engined One-Eleven, but considers that for the -500 Series in airline usage, the balance would almost certainly have been positive in favour of re-engining.

There are, of course, other important reasons for re-engining - such as noise reduction. This was certainly a crucial factor in the case for One-Eleven re-engining. The importance of achieving Stage 3 noise levels may be greater than seeking a positive economic case. The noise situation is discussed below.

Noise

A full range of noise measurements and testing at certification conditions was undertaken. Permitted noise levels at the three flights conditions required for certification to FAR Part 36, Stage 3, are tabulated below, together with the levels predicted beforehand for the Dee Howard -400 Series aircraft and the actual measured levels. While the certification levels are the ones that matter, the predicted levels are important because they are quoted in the initial pre-flight sales brochures and may be used as the basis of guarantees.

BAC One-Eleven -400 series with Tay 650 engines
Max take-off weight - 91,500 lb; max landing weight - 82,000 lb

Effective perceived noise levels (EPNdB)

Flight Condition	FAR Part 36 Stage 3 limit	Pre-Flight Prediction	Certification Levels (rel. to limits)
Sideline	94.6	93.2	92.0 (-2.6)
Flyover (cutback)	89.0	83.0	82.0 (-7.0)
Approach	98.6	92.0	91.6 (-7.0)

It will be noted that sideline noise levels are closer to the Stage 3 limits than with flyover or approach. This is because of the dominance of jet noise at sideline, which in turn is a function of the jet velocity. The Tay's jet velocity is a little higher than on other modern turbofans because its bypass ratio of 3 is somewhat lower than that of the bigger transport engines like the RB211 or Trent. A heavier weight Tay-powered -500 Series One-Eleven, if it had been developed would have had a lower flyover noise margin and slightly greater margin at sideline, due to higher take-off speed.

Emissions

The subject of Tay combustion emissions did not attract a great deal of notice during the various marketing campaigns for re-engining or new aircraft production, but in fact the story is very good. Perhaps it should be explained here that it is quite impractical to measure emissions for individual aircraft. The procedure for certification is that one, or better still, two or three engines are tested and probability theory used to estimate the average fleet-wide emissions for an engine.

The emissions for the Tay and the Spey are shown on the chart below. It will be seen that Spey emissions of the pollutants carbon monoxide and unburnt hydrocarbons far exceed the limits set by the International Civil Aviation Organisation (ICAO). The Tay engine emissions are well beneath the limits on all pollutants.

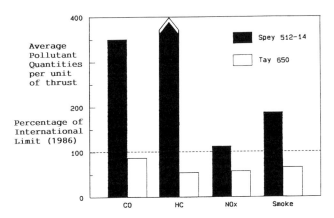

Comparison of Spey 512-14 and Tay 650 emissions levels

CHAPTER SIX

Prototype flying and renewed marketing activity

Soon after the first flight of the prototype re-engined One-Eleven aircraft, the flight development and certification programme commenced. However, the need to pursue firm sales was given top priority by the Aeritalia Board and in support of this, arrangements were made to exhibit the aircraft at the Farnborough Air Show, at the beginning of September 1990, even though the absence of the aircraft from San Antonio would inevitably delay the already-late flight certification programme.

The Dee Howard One-Eleven visits the UK

Birmingham Airport, England, was at the time, having to commit a permanent team to deal with the local community about noise complaints. The airport, therefore, welcomed a suggestion that the Dee Howard One-Eleven should undertake a series of noise tests at the airport, on its way to Farnborough. The noise survey, which took place on 28 August, utilised existing airport noise monitors, though only one of these, about four miles from the take-off point gave good comparable results. Two flights by the Tay-powered One-Eleven were compared with a number of flights by Spey-powered One-Elevens, all of which were operated by British Airways or Birmingham European Airways aircraft. Aircraft weights, where recorded, were not exactly similar but the noise recordings highlighted the startling reduction in flyover noise of the Tay aircraft against the Spey-powered aircraft. The chart below records the results.

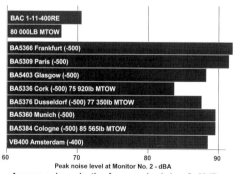

BAC 1-11-400 with Tay 650 engines - Flyover noise measurements at Birmingham Airport

Birmingham Airport noise measurements

68

After these flights at Birmingham, with their eminently marketable results, the Dee Howard aircraft went to Farnborough and flew demonstration flights at the Air Show, (see photographs overleaf).

The quietness of the aircraft was noted by the public and commentators. One worrying feature, fortunately not highlighted by the press but noted by observers, was that the tailplane was seen to shake quite noticeably in full reverse thrust landings. Clearly the efflux from the upper thrust reverser doors was so directed that it was buffeting the tailplane.

An interesting postscript to the Birmingham flights occurred during a meeting between Rolls-Royce and Aeritalia personnel on the Aeritalia stand at the Farnborough Air Show. A group of Birmingham-based British Airways pilots and operations personnel appeared and sought an opportunity to explain that they were worried about the noise of the Spey-powered One-Eleven in the BA fleet and concerned that they were going to have imposed on them a replacement fleet of Boeing 737-200s which were being discarded by BA at Heathrow. They were not happy about this but had heard about the excellent noise results of the re-engined aircraft and asked for a study to be done to make the case for the One-Elevens to be retained and re-engined.

Associated Aerospace - serious problems emerge

It was also in the early autumn of 1990 that the first cracks in the optimistic external outlook of Associated Aerospace started to appear. Obtaining a credible source of funding had been a continual problem and also in mid-August Managing Director Brian Kyme reported to Rolls-Royce his difficulty in arranging for the Dee Howard nacelles to be supplied through BAe. This link was not working and Kyme was striving to set up a link directly with Aeritalia. The situation really started worsening for AAe at the Farnborough Air Show in early September 1990. Here at a meeting between Rolls-Royce's Charles Cuddington and two senior officials of the Romanian Ministry of Resources and Industry, the Romanians stated that *"the AAe contract would not proceed"*. The reason admitted by the Director of the Aircraft Factory, General Smirnov, was that the aircraft price *"would not cover the salaries of the factory"*. At a follow-on meeting the Minister himself re-iterated that the deal would not happen. The Romanian's ambition was *"not to be a supplier of sub-assemblies but to sell complete aircraft"*.

Despite these forebodings, Associated Aerospace announced at Farnborough that it had appointed Lovaux Ltd of Hurn Airport (already mentioned earlier) as the completion centre for the new AAe One-Eleven programme. Lovaux would become project leader in all matters relating to aircraft completion and would take an equity position in AAe. At this time

The Dee Howard Tay/One-Eleven about to land at Farnborough

The landing run with thrust reversers deployed

Lovaux was a subsidiary company of FLS Aerospace and had a major capability for the maintenance and overhaul of BAC One-Elevens, with a significant customer list.

In October, and in confirmation of the Farnborough rumours, the Romanians were perceived by AAe to be delaying their signature of the contract with AAe. However, at the end of November 1990 there was yet another disturbing development. Two representatives from the Paris office of Coopers & Lybrand - the well-known accountancy and financial services company - visited Rolls-Royce and British Aerospace. One was from the Paris Office, the other an American. They claimed that Coopers & Lybrand had been retained by the Romanian Government to advise on the viability of the AAe project. In reality, the pair appear to have been asked to prepare a case for the Romanians to walk away from the programme. In an interview with the author their line of questioning was quite hostile, with the American asking the question, *"How could you guys invest in such a nutty deal?"*

Subsequently, the author spoke to the Paris-based Coopers & Lybrand representative. He reluctantly admitted that they had given a poor report on the AAe programme. A telephone conversation with AAe's Brian Kyme revealed another aspect of this unfavourable situation. According to Kyme, BAe, in its interview with the Coopers & Lybrand team had decided to underplay the AAe programme and denied having any contract with AAe or reveal that they had a 'Heads of Agreement'. By all accounts the American interviewer had at all meetings been abrasive and rude.

More seriously, the Romanian authorities were now uncooperative and refused to sign the AAe Contract. Additionally there was no willingness to release Ship 409 to the Dee Howard Company for use in a certification programme. Brian Kyme blamed the situation on a combination of bureaucracy and the failure of the Romanian regime in Bucharest to come to terms with western business concepts.

Dee Howard's marketing continues

Towards the end of the year, the Dee Howard Company referred to only three firm sales; the Dee Howard aircraft, HM Industries - a US affiliate of the UK Hanson Trust - and Turbo-Union, which is the management company of Rolls-Royce, MTU and Fiat Aviazone which produces engines for the three-nation Tornado aircraft.

The business of selling to HM Industries had caused some friction between Rolls-Royce and the Dee Howard Company. Dee Howard intended to use this aircraft as a second prototype, in order to test the new Honeywell cockpit avionics suite and had made a substantial discount on the price for re-engining to compensate for the aircraft being out of service for so long.

As a consequence, Dee Howard came to Rolls-Royce to seek a generous discount on engine price but Rolls-Royce refused to budge from an earlier offer of 9%. Aeritalia complained to Rolls-Royce's Managing Director that this was unreasonably niggardly.

Also showing interest in the programme was Birmingham European Airways which operated five -400 Series aircraft. An Aeritalia and Rolls-Royce visit was made at which a conversion price of $8.5m per aircraft was mentioned. BEA asked if any UK company would be licensed to undertake conversions, for example, Lovaux of Hurn.

A trickle of enquiries was also received at this time from the UK's Ministry of Defence (Procurement Executive), about the possible use of the re-engined One-Eleven for a VIP flight. The need was for an aircraft (a) with unrestricted capability to fly from London to Washington and (b) to have as much UK content as possible. Almost certainly this aircraft would be earmarked for the Royal Flight. Rather as Derek Lowe had earlier predicted, the -400 Series aircraft, with barely 3000 nm range was inadequate, but if it was available, the -500 Series, fitted with Tay engines and Cranfield's long-range fuel tanks would carry out the task comfortably. Unfortunately, -500 Series re-engining had not yet been launched and Dee Howard had furthermore requested to Rolls-Royce a delay in the delivery of a ship-set of engines for a -500 certification programme.

As the end of the year approached, a sense of urgency bordering on desperation, was creeping into Aeritalia/Dee Howard's marketing activity. It was decided that it really must try to secure five firm orders from US corporate operators before the end of 1990 and approached Rolls-Royce to give a 10% discount on the engine prices for these aircraft.

This was agreed. Nine operators were actually targeted. Of these, Avjet, which had previously paid a deposit, decided to pull out because it was so disillusioned with Dee Howard's slow progress. Montex Drilling said it would not get interested until the Dee Howard Company had obtained the Supplemental Type Certificate. Four other operators were willing to receive proposals, Louisana Pacific, Huizenga Holdings, The Coastal Corporation and Amway.

In the course of this targeted campaign it was reported by Dee Howard sales personnel that,

"a dominant theme is emerging from these first contacts (sic) with BAC 1-11-400 corporate operators and that is they all want increased range for the aircraft, ie more range than the predicted 3,050 nm. In order to have an even chance of being successful in the corporate market we must do everything possible to get a 3,200 to 3,600 nm range."

Once again this raised the question as to whether the -500 Series, or -475 Series would have been a better baseline aircraft for conversion to a quiet long-range corporate jet.

An additional feedback from the sales tour was a questioning of the need to upgrade the cockpit avionics so extensively and whether there was adequate cost benefit from this upgrade.

In association with this specific sales initiative, the Dee Howard Company engaged a well-known business jet marketing company called James Markel and Associates, to *"assist with more energetic and wider-based sales effort on the One-Eleven"*.

NewBAC

At long last, in November, Aeritalia produced a business plan for the NewBAC proposal. The essence was that NewBAC would have four shareholders with the following shares division:

Electra (a leasing company)	40%
Aeritalia	30%
Credit Italiano	20%
Rolls-Royce	10%

The company would have an equity of $50m. It was expected that the total cost of buying the 34 aircraft from BA would be $80m and that BA would lease the aircraft back - still with Spey engines - until they were ready to be re-engined. Initial estimates which assumed a lease rate of $150,000 per month and a residual value of $4m per aircraft (both rather optimistic), produced an internal rate of return of 13.5%, somewhat below the target of 20%.

In due course the NewBAC proposal drifted away. It is believed that Aeritalia was not impressed with the projected internal rate of return, nor about Rolls-Royce's insistence that it would not accept a negative cash flow.

Increasing programme strains

A further strain on the programme was a deterioration in the commercial relationship between Rolls-Royce and the Dee Howard Company. Of the most immediate concern was the procrastination and unwillingness of Dee Howard to pay the balance of nearly $3m for the second pair of Tay engines for the flight programme of the second prototype aircraft. These were ready to be dispatched on contract in December 1990 but despite the pressure on Dee Howard from a succession of representations from Rolls-Royce higher

73

management, no money was forthcoming.

Another continuing concern on the commercial side between Rolls-Royce and the Dee Howard Company over this period was the delay in the decision whether to launch the -500 Series re-engine programme and an unwillingness to confirm the order for the first three ship-sets of production engines. With no sign of significant re-engine orders, Dee Howard clearly did not want to commit to buying the engines.

Development and certification flying

Meanwhile, the flight test programme was continuing and by mid-November about 90 hours of flying had been logged. Perhaps this is a suitable point to outline the nature of the flight certification programme as set out by British Aerospace, the design authority.

All flights were carried out under a BAe Design Clearance, signed off by BAe's Chief Engineer (Roger Back) and all certification flying had a BAe captain (either John Lewis or John Fawcett). Any other flying could have a Dee Howard crew (headed by Ron Franzen), approved by BAe. The flight programme had to be agreed by BAe's resident representative in San Antonio (Chris King). The test requirements of the American FAA and the British CAA were slightly different and the flight programme covered both certification requirements.

Also in November the latest Rolls-Royce appointee to the position of Head of the Tay Project, John Sadler, visited San Antonio and observed

(a)   that the programme seemed to be slipping day-by-day

(b)   that the prototype aircraft was over 20 years old and had been poorly maintained in its earlier life. Every attempt to continue the flight programme was met by new aircraft problems, particularly in the aircraft systems

(c)   he felt that Aeritalia had a lack of enthusiasm for the project.

On 16 November yet another short delay was caused when an engine nacelle access panel blew off in flight causing a secondary hole in the nacelle's skin. More serious was an incident in early December when one of the thrust reversers went into uncommanded reverse thrust during engine run-up. Possible causes initially suspected were that the thrust reverser had been rigged incorrectly or that there were electrical control circuit problems. Fortunately there was no repetition of this problem.

At a meeting with the Federal Aviation Administration the lack of preparation of the technical manuals was revealed. The Dee Howard Company realised that the manuals would not be ready in time by Dee Howard activity alone and requested British Aerospace to undertake this work. BAe agreed in the interim but was expected to charge a high price for its assistance.

Finally at the turn of the year, Aeritalia, having merged with a large Italian electronics company, became known as Alenia.

CHAPTER SEVEN

The end of the Dee Howard programme

The marketing of the Dee Howard re-engining programme was reviewed yet again in January 1991 at a meeting between Alenia (formerly Aeritalia) seniors, led by Renzo Lunardi and Rolls-Royce led by Charles Cuddington. It was reported that none of the corporate customers targeted before Christmas had signed up for the discounted proposals. Alenia expressed some irritation that the marketing programme had not made better progress and even muttered darkly about the bad consequences of a possible cancellation.

It is not surprising that the US corporate customers did not rush forward to place orders for their One-Elevens to be re-engined. It was seven years previously that they had first expressed such interest in the re-engining!

One can also understand Alenia's general concerns about the market. Six Tay/One-Eleven campaigns or initiatives had been undertaken during the previous year and none had yielded any positive results. A summary of these activities is as follows:

*   **Associated Aerospace** - announced a programme launch but found the Romanian's back-pedalling with their support. The programme looked under threat.

*   **GPA** - withdrew its interest despite previous enthusiasm for a large -500 Series re-engining order. Blamed potential market overcapacity.

*   **Helijet** - never seemed to be a credible customer for a 50-aircraft order but attracted a great deal of Dee Howard attention.

*   **The Jaffe Group** - showed great enthusiasm for re-engining during a flag-waving visit to Bucharest but no evidence of serious follow through.

*   **NewBAC** - A brave idea to kick-start a large leasing programme with aircraft purchased from BA but a superficial view of the economics did not encourage.

*   The late-1990 special deal to US corporate operators did not attract enough interest and was probably too late in the day.

Quite apart from this gloomy picture there had been the distraction of an announcement by the Romanians of a Spey hush kit programme!

The market review meeting continued with a discussion on the prospects for sales to four European One-Eleven operators. These were the Ford Motor Company of Europe, which used three -400 Series aircraft on a shuttle operation between sites, Birmingham European Airways (also a -400 Series operator), the Ministry of Defence and Salian, the company originally formed by the late Sheikh Salem Binladen and Ian Munro.

Notwithstanding the fact that it had been discussing with customers the re-engining of the -500 Series aircraft, the Dee Howard company wrote to Rolls-Royce to say that it did not intend to make a decision on re-engining and certificating this Series until the end of 1991 and wanted to delay any decision on the delivery of the first six production Tay engines (for the existing -400 Series programme) until June.

In view of the failure to attract any US corporate customers during its 1990 special sales initiative, Dee Howard company conducted some further discussions with the Jaffe Group, which was in the business of upgrading large corporate aircraft and whose visit to Romania in the spring of 1990 was discussed earlier. Nothing seemed to come of these discussions; there were rumours of Jaffe hoping to achieve a very high price for any such re-engined aircraft - perhaps as much as $13m for the conversion.

The collapse of Associated Aerospace

In February, Associated Aerospace was taken to court by creditors for unsettled expenses including unpaid public relations fees. It had no significant assets in order to pay and the company went into liquidation. The creditors claimed the personal securities that had been put up by the AAe Directors.

Sadly with the collapse of the company went the opportunity of launching an imaginative programme which could have put fresh life into the Romanian production of One-Eleven aircraft and created useful business for BAe, Rolls-Royce and the other suppliers.

Lovaux

While activity was intensifying in San Antonio, interest in One-Eleven re-engining had not totally died in the UK. It will be remembered that Lovaux of Hurn had expressed interest in the concept as early as 1988; in June 1991 the author was asked to meet Ed Searle, who was Sales and Marketing Director of both Lovaux and Dan-Air Engineering of Lasham, Hampshire. By this time, Lovaux was no longer independent and with Dan-Air

Engineering had been bought by FLS Aerospace, a company owned by the Danish conglomerate FLS.

Lovaux had earlier been selected by the now defunct Associated Aerospace to fit out the bare Romanian One-Eleven airframes which were going to be manufactured under that programme. With the AAe programme dead, Lovaux was now looking at alternative ways of using its expertise on the One-Eleven to get into the re-engining programme. Searle had heard rumours that Alenia was prepared to sell the re-engine programme and he was keen to meet Alenia to discuss such a possibility. Lovaux was also keen to buy the design authority for the One-Eleven from BAe but the latter had refused to consider the matter, presumably still fearing a potential development of the One-Eleven which might present competition for the BAe 146 airliner. Searle subsequently tried to arrange a meeting with Alenia to try to secure some level of Lovaux participation in the Alenia re-engining programme.

As noted earlier, Lovaux had the contract to service at least seven Middle Eastern-owned One-Elevens. Ed Searle indicated that Galeb Binladen, a brother of the late Salem Binladen, had expressed interest in having his aircraft re-engined but had been quoted a price by Dee Howard *'which took no account of the contributions to the re-engine programme which had been made by his brother'*.

Certification flying

During the Spring of 1991 a number of certification milestones were successfully achieved. These included aft centre-of-gravity stall testing to both FAA and CAA requirements and aircraft field performance tests (take-off and landing) which took place at Roswell, New Mexico. Additionally, noise certification testing took place at Moses Lake, Washington, yielding excellent margins relative to Federal regulations FAR Part 36. These results were illustrated in a previous chapter.

However, during the flight testing some unexpected problems had emerged. The first was the effect of the jet exhaust shaking the tailplane when the aircraft engaged full reverse thrust, a problem which had been noticed at Farnborough. Strain gauge testing had indicated that tailplane loads exceeded British Aerospace's specified limits. All certification flying after the Farnborough experience was conducted at restricted reverse thrust power levels. Four solutions were being considered:

(a) clocking round the thrust reverser buckets, (though there was doubt whether this would be sufficient)

(b) strengthening the tailplane assembly, (this was likely to result in such a degree of change as be outside the scope of a Supplemental Type Certificate)

(c) attaching vanes to the thrust reverser buckets to direct the exhaust plume away, (this would mean some redesign of the thrust reverser and require some of the already-completed thrust reverser testing behind the engine to be repeated),

(d) do nothing immediately and certificate the aircraft with the thrust reverser operating only at engine idling thrust (referred to by some as an 'aluminium parachute'!); then make changes to the thrust reverser and gain a further Supplemental Type Certificate later.

Whatever course was chosen it was somewhat optimistically hoped that certification of the aircraft could be achieved at the latest by September 1991.

Question marks about the safety characteristics of the Tay's Dee Howard thrust reverser were raised by the outcome of the investigation into the crash of a Lauda Air Boeing 767 aircraft, which showed that a thrust reverser had opened in flight. It was expected that there would be more stringent checks on the adequacy of thrust reverser locking mechanisms, but informed opinion was that the Dee Howard reverser design was inherently extremely safe.

The second unexpected certification problem was that the aircraft failed its initial wet runway water ingestion testing. Among solutions considered for this was an alternative design of tyre with a chine to improve spray deflection.

Problems were also experienced with the engine's acceleration characteristics, particularly with need to resolve the conflicting requirements of speedy 'go-around' and surge-free rapid handling at altitude.

An increasing concern for the completion of the certification programme, as perceived by Alenia, was the slow pace of BAe's activity, as design authority, to provide the structural justification or approval of modifications, which was due at the end of August.

The FAA

It had been decided by Alenia to try to certificate the aircraft through the Federal Aviation Administration's office in Seattle, using the services of a local company, Shannon Engineering. The original certification of the

One-Eleven aircraft had been conducted to the British Civil Airworthiness Requirements (BCAR) and cross-certificated by the FAA by an established paperwork route. The intention was for the re-engined aircraft to gain a US Supplemental Type Certificate (STC), but with hindsight, BAe's Chief Engineer feels that it was unwise to seek an STC for an aircraft which was not originally certificated in the USA. Although the -400 Series aircraft type had originally received an FAA certificate, the -500 Series aircraft had not. Thus while the first aim was to gain FAA certification for the re-engined -400 Series, it was also intended to achieve a British CAA certificate and certain additional tests were put into the flight programme to facilitate this.

It was soon apparent that the FAA was virtually treating the re-engine programme as though it was a new aircraft, rather than just a Supplemental Type Certificate. To deal with the re-engined One-Eleven certification, the FAA assigned a relatively inexperienced engineer, who insisted on working the certification process to the letter of 'the book'. The result was that, because the One-Eleven was not a US product, the engineer called for ever more background data, particularly on structural matters, from the original 1960's certification

These demands were passed by Alenia to BAe, who claimed that the process was not helped by delays in Alenia passing on the requests. BAe's willingness to help was no doubt tempered by the fact that these additional data requests were probably not covered by the original Technical Assistance Agreement and it was rumoured that Alenia/Dee Howard owed BAe a backlog of fees. BAe itself found it increasingly difficult to find the data among 25-year-old files and drawings. (Remember also that all One-Eleven data had to be moved to Bristol when the Weybridge factory closed down.)

Witnessing this situation, Jon Taylor, the resident Rolls-Royce Flight Test Manager in San Antonio, concluded that FAA Certification could not be expected before the end of November 1991.

It had been hoped that the certification process would be speeded up by the conversion of a second One-Eleven -400 Series aircraft, that owned by HM Industries, (ship number 076, serial number N333GB) but ground running in June 1991 had been held up by late delivery of aircraft modifications. In the rush to get the aircraft converted, the paperwork which related approved drawings and the parts actually installed had got badly out of step. Sorting this out was not helped by the first signs of the impact on engineering personnel of being divided between two programmes, the BAC One-Eleven and the Boeing 727-100 re-engine programme.

The storm clouds gather

At the Dee Howard Company meanwhile, President and Chief Operating Officer Phil Greco, had left the Company, together with VP Business Development Steve Townes and Sales Manager Rick Oehme and there was nobody left on the sales and marketing side of the One-Eleven programme. In Europe, the Resident Rolls-Royce Manager with Turbo-Union, Doug Harpley, had picked up a rumour that Alenia had decided to cancel the re-engine programme after the conversion of the Turbo-Union aircraft, which was due to be inducted into San Antonio in August.

At another meeting between Charles Cuddington and Renzo Lunardi, at the end of July, Rolls-Royce was told that Alenia had decided to stop the programme after the certification of the -400 Series aircraft. Lunardi further said that Alenia was prepared to sell the One-Eleven re-engine programme for $50m.

At San Antonio, a senior contracts official expressed the opinion that no-one would sign up for the programme until the Supplemental Type Certificate had been gained and performance numbers established. On this latter subject there was concern at Rolls-Royce that the projected 17% improvement in range may have been eroded by higher-than-expected weight and drag from the Tay powerplant and higher than acceptable nacelle leakages and engine bleed flows. The real performance situation would only be established by properly conducted flight testing and measurement, but unfortunately this had been omitted from the original Dee Howard contract.

A sinister new development in an increasingly sensitive situation became apparent at the end of August when the new Chief Operating Officer of the Dee Howard Company, Matthew Donohue, cancelled a proposed visit to Turbo-Union. He claimed that this was unfortunately due to his inability to give Turbo-Union a credible date for the certification of their aircraft, because in turn Dee Howard had been continually hampered in its efforts to obtain that certification by the failure of British Aerospace to provide the pertinent data required for the certification. (This was the first time this claim had been made publicly).

Certification - the final struggles

On the flight certification programme, by mid-September, the prototype aircraft had completed testing at Roswell, New Mexico, to certificate reverse thrust landings at approach idle engine settings (to obviate the tailplane shaking problem) and analysis of tailplane structural loads was awaited from BAe. Senior Alenia management mentioned to Rolls-Royce at a meeting on another subject that they saw three major problems still to be resolved, horizontal stabiliser (tailplane) stress, water ingestion from wet runways and anti-icing control. Alenia was known to be reviewing the viability of the programme.

Although the first prototype aircraft was due to fly to Seattle for the FAA Certification Review in early November, there were continuing delays caused by the need to sort out a number of smaller snags. The second prototype meanwhile had had a very successful programme of flying and testing Honeywell's new avionics suite at its facility at Phoenix. However, rumours were spreading in the Dee Howard facility of the imminent termination of the programme.

The impending crisis for the Dee Howard programme was forewarned by a message from Rolls-Royce's Jon Taylor on 5 November. The first two paragraphs of this message, with slight amendment for clarification were as follows:

"Despite the optimism evinced by Shannon Engineering last week, new and major obstacles to the issue of a Type Inspection Approval (TIA) became apparent late on Friday. These are due to concerns on the part of the FAA structural specialists in Seattle, over the BAe structural justification for the modification. It is hard to understand how this can suddenly become an issue now, when BAe made a firm commitment to conclude the analysis and furnish the Dee Howard Company with reports by August 31st 1991. It is also reported that the additional work required, on the part of BAe, may generate commercial considerations which could further impact the conclusion of this work.

The upshot of this is the re-definition of the One-Eleven certification programme, as of last night, to show the TIA issue in the New Year. FAA flight testing cannot start until after issue of the TIA."

On Friday 8 November 1991 and despite a great deal of head-scratching to see if CAA certification could be obtained more quickly than with the FAA - who would be unlikely to issue a TIA before January 1992 - it was announced by Dee Howard management to its staff that all further flying to achieve CAA Certification was cancelled. However, despite the termination of the quest for CAA flight certification and gradual withdrawal of personnel from the programme, flying continued in pursuit of FAA certification on both prototype aircraft. On 13 November, Flight 178, on the first prototype, to demonstrate a modified pylon drainage arrangement, was successfully completed. This turned out to be the last flight of this aircraft.

At a meeting on the 13th the Dee Howard Director of Flight Test and Certification, Bill Hurley, explained to his team that the principal hang-up on structural certification was the analysis of load margins. A major difficulty was the way in which the structures data was analysed and presented 20 years previously at the time of the original certification compared with current methods. BAe had agreed to supply further data on this margins analysis but it would not be available until January 1992. The FAA would not issue a TIA before this date. This delay would have a significant impact on the attempts to complete the certification programme. It was also revealed that flight data acquisition equipment was due to be removed from the One-Eleven before the end of January in order to be re-installed in the prototype re-engined Boeing 727-100.

The recently appointed VP Engineering at San Antonio, Attilio Galasso, seconded from Alenia in Italy, reviewed the programme and quickly concluded that the problems with the structural analysis lay entirely with BAe and claimed that the analysis was at least a year late in being supplied to the FAA.

During the week of 18 November, the first prototype re-engined aircraft, constructor number (c/n) 059 was parked in a closed hangar and the Tay engines prepared for short term storage. The second prototype, c/n 076 was similarly grounded at Phoenix.

HM Industries was informed that there would be an indefinite delay to the return of their aircraft. The company's comments on this were not reported. Arrangements for compensation were not discussed.

BAC1-11 Series 400 with Tay 650-14 Programme achievements

- Massive reductions in noise relative to Stage 2 Spey-powered aircraft — almost 30dB cumulative reduction

- Noise margins below Stage 3 of 2.6dB at sideline, 7.0dB at cutback-flyover, and 7.3dB at approach.

- Very large reductions in combustion emissions

- Two aircraft flown — total of over 300 flying hours

- No engine concerns

- Extension of aircraft operating envelope to 41 000 ft

- Successful operation and safety demonstration of Dee Howard thrust reversers

At the time of cessation of the flight programme, the first prototype had flown for 337.9 hours and the second prototype, 97.4 hours.

As the programme closed, the achievements listed above were claimed. Note no mention of performance improvements - because they were never measured!

After the end of the programme

News of the suspension of the Dee Howard BAC One-Eleven re-engining programme did not come to the notice of the media until about 5 December 1991, when the journal *Flight International* telephoned Rolls-Royce Inc in the USA to say that several Dee Howard employees had been in touch with the magazine, some anonymously, to report the problems with the re-engining programme and to cast doubt on the progress with the much bigger programme to re-engine the Boeing 727-100s of United Parcel Service. The immediate reaction of Rolls-Royce was to play down any impact on the 727 programme, the first prototype flight of which was not due to fly until the early Spring.

The suspension of the re-engining programme became public in the *Flight International* issue of 11-17 December. In this article, an Alenia spokesperson described the programme as being *"temporarily frozen for technical and bureaucratic reasons"*. Elsewhere in the article a Dee Howard senior executive said that the freeze was because

"...we've had difficulty getting support for the STC. A lot of money has already been spent without the necessary support from certification authorities and suppliers. Rolls-Royce has been fine, we have no complaints there, but it goes into other areas. It's a sad scenario because we were so close, but it is an expensive contract to continue when you don't get support."

The article alleged that $80m had been spent on the programme. This was neither confirmed nor denied by Dee Howard.

The lawsuits

Alenia commenced legal proceedings against British Aerospace alleging negligence, delays and refusal to release information. (The court petition, File Number 91-C1-17199, was filed at Bexar County Court, in San Antonio, on 4 December 1991). BAe expressed surprise at this turn of events and claimed that it had not turned down any calls for help. *Flight International* suggested that there was a belief that BAe had been reluctant to release the necessary data because the One-Eleven programme might provide unwelcome competition to its efforts to sell its current production 90- to 100-seat regional aircraft, the BAe146.

Dee Howard's case can be summarised as follows. Although BAe had assured Dee Howard that it was willing and able to perform and discharge its obligations, it was Dee Howard's complaint that BAe was in fact unable and unwilling to do so and that BAe's representations *were made with reckless disregard if not outright knowledge of their falsity*. Dee Howard further claimed that BAe never intended to fulfil its assurances and promises which were made with the intent of collecting substantial payments from Dee Howard and delaying the re-engine programme as long as possible; in particular that BAe failed to prepare, analyse and produce loads, method verification and structure substantiation or justification data for the Dee Howard Company to send onwards to the FAA and that it was because of BAe's failure to deliver on time all the contracted data that the FAA withheld timely issuance of a TIA or STC for the re-engined One-Eleven.

On 19 December, Rolls-Royce was formally advised that the One-Eleven re-engining programme was cancelled and that the Dee Howard Company had filed a lawsuit against BAe, claiming damages. Dee Howard also said again that it would return the first prototype's two engines to Rolls-Royce and would not take title to them. Rolls-Royce replied to say again that there was no unilateral provision in the contract for Dee Howard to cancel the orders. It was only possible either to pay for the engines or pay cancellation charges.

A separate report indicated that HM Industries had filed a lawsuit against Alenia for failing to fulfil its contract on aircraft c/n 076. Evidently the contract obliged Dee Howard to pay $100,000 for each month that the programme was late.

Another aggrieved party was Turbo-Union, which had already bought two Tay 650 engines direct from Rolls-Royce. Turbo-Union was a consortium of engine manufacturers which consisted of Rolls-Royce, MTU of Germany and the Italian engine company, Fiat Aviazione, which manufactured the RB199 engines for the British/German/Italian Tornado aircraft. Turbo-Union's customer was the NATO Agency of the governments of the three countries, known by the acronym NAMMA.

The Tornado aircraft itself was also built by a British/German/Italian consortium of which the British and Italian manufacturers were respectively BAe and Alenia. When the One-Eleven re-engining programme was cancelled and Turbo-Union found itself out of pocket, NAMMA took up the matter with Alenia through consortium channels and ensured direct compensation from Alenia for Turbo-Union's debts.

It was just at this time when lawsuits were being filed that Matt Donohue was promoted from COO to President of the Dee Howard Company.

A further lawsuit was filed by Ian Munro, as Administrator of the Estate of Sheikh Salem Binladen and Salian International, claiming that they funded the Dee Howard Company to launch the programme, that Dee Howard had used the technology that was developed for the One-Eleven to its advantage on the Boeing 727 re-engine programme and that they had done this without compensating Sheikh Binladen and Salian and were now breaking several agreements by stopping the programme. The agreements broken were that the Dee Howard Company did not establish a separate BAC One-Eleven Re-engine Company, did not repay Salem Binladen's investment, failed to keep him informed on the status of the programme, failed to tell him that Dee Howard was selling the entire programme to Alenia and falsely represented that there was no transfer of technology, experience and data from the BAC One-Eleven to the Boeing 727 (re-engining) programme.

From this point on, the corpse of the Dee Howard One-Eleven programme was picked over in the offices of the various lawyers representing Dee Howard, BAe, Salian, Turbo-Union and HM Industries but little emerged into the light of day. An interesting update was provided on November 1992, nearly a year after the stoppage of the programme, by the Rolls-Royce local commercial representative in Italy, who happened also to represent British Aerospace. He reported that the Alenia corporate headquarters function was in a state of disarray, with the auditors unwilling to audit the books because of the liabilities represented by the lawsuits against its subsidiaries.

Thus four lawsuits had been filed: Dee Howard vs British Aerospace; British Aerospace vs Dee Howard; Salian vs Dee Howard and HM Industries vs Dee Howard. Of these four, that being pursued by Hanson Trust on behalf of its affiliated company, HM Industries seemed to be the most pressing problem. To try to resolve some of the problems, the Managing Director of Alenia Aircraft Group, Roberto Mannu, wanted Alenia and BAe 'experts' to meet, but BAe refused this request. It was claimed that Alenia owed BAe $6m of unpaid fees under the Technical Assistance Agreement. The MD of Alenia also wished to meet his opposite number at BAe, but this was declined unless Alenia withdrew its lawsuit against BAe. This was refused.

A Paris Air Show meeting

Despite the litigation still continuing into 1993, a major twist to the story occurred on 15 June when the Managing Directors of Rolls-Royce Aerospace Group (John Sandford), British Aerospace, Airbus Division (Bob

86

McKinlay) and Alenia's Aircraft Modification Group (Nino d'Angelo) and their supporting staffs held a meeting at the Paris Air Show. The meeting was triggered by the active interest of the Romanians in re-commencing new production of One-Elevens with Tay engines. However, the discussion concentrated instead on trying to re-activate the Alenia/Dee Howard One-Eleven -400 Series re-engine programme and little reference was made to the Romanian programme. BAe surprised the meeting by saying it would consider the completion of the -400 Series re-engining programme but would need a front-end financial contribution from Rolls-Royce of about $5m. Alenia, led by Nino d'Angelo, considered that such completion would take about a year and would cost $10-15m. Rolls-Royce agreed to make a financial concession towards the re-start of the re-engine programme but made it conditional on BAe supporting the Romanian programme. This condition was not well received by BAe.

At a follow-up meeting between BAe and Rolls-Royce, BAe outlined its view of how the certification of the -400 could be achieved, with BAe taking charge of the programme and Alenia/Dee Howard providing an aircraft (almost certainly the second prototype) and other services. BAe stated that it would not support the Romanian programme unless the -400 re-engine programme was settled first. A list was presented, of items needing to be undertaken to complete the certification and a tentative programme. This is shown below.

**BAC One-Eleven -400 re-engining;
estimate of tasks remaining to complete certification**

* Complete drawings (update 250 drawings out of 1200)
* Complete reports (20 revisions or new issues)
* Testing:
    Fire extinguishing
    Pylon-cooling
    Water ingestion
    Pneumatic system
    Anti-ice
    Drainage
    Thrust Reverser development, if necessary
* Fatigue and damage tolerance (fatigue test of engine attachment)
* Component qualification tests (only a few, if 727RE components are used)
* Manuals (Aircraft Flight Manual, Maintenance Manual)
* Prepare aircraft for flight test

Provisional programme

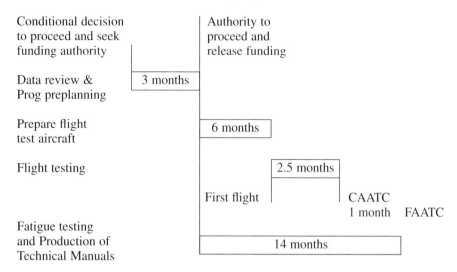

Rolls-Royce responded to another demand for $5m contribution to re-launch the programme by offering $0.25m per aircraft for 10 aircraft, but dependent on firm orders for 11 shipsets of Tay engines for the Romanian programme. BAe responded that it did not consider this concession to be adequate and didn't like the fact that it was linked to the Romanian programme! This was hypocritical in as much as BAe was linking its own support of the Romanians as conditional on the certification of the Dee Howard programme.

However, in August 1993, a report was received from San Antonio that the Alenia court case against BAe had been listed for trial in November 1994. This was perceived as taking the pressure off BAe from having to support the completion of the -400 Series re-engine programme and thereby extending the slow death of all One-Eleven/Tay activity.

Lawsuits resolved

At the beginning of October it was reported in the press (see for example *Flight International* of 5 October 1992) that the Bexar County Court in San Antonio had found in favour of Salian International, also representing the estate of Salem Binladen, after a six week court hearing.

It was reported that, in the judgement, the estate of Salem Binladen and

Salian International had been awarded damages of approximately $5m for breach of the contract signed by the Dee Howard Company at the 1987 Paris Air Show. The argument was that Dee Howard had failed to establish a separate company for the re-engining programme and which would have converted the £995,000 loaned by Binladen into a 20% investment in such a company. It was judged that Sheikh Binladen's investment was crucial in persuading Rolls-Royce to commit to the programme and that the technology gained from the launch of the BAC One-Eleven programme helped Dee Howard secure the $400m UPS contract for re-engining of the Boeing 727.

Following the above settlement, it was reported by BAe in February 1994 that the litigation between BAe and Alenia had been settled, but no details were given.

As detailed earlier, Hanson Industries Inc, on behalf of HM Industries, sued the Dee Howard Company for breach of contract. This case was also settled out of court, the sum of $6.5m being mentioned in the press and all damages recovered.

A curious postscript to the whole Dee Howard One-Eleven re-engining programme was provided by the *Derby Evening Telegraph*, the local newspaper for the Derby area of England, where the Rolls-Royce Company concentrates its commercial aero-engine work. To accompany an article on 24 January 1995, about holiday charter flights from United Kingdom airports, the newspaper provided a photograph of the first prototype, Dee Howard re-engined One-Eleven - an experimental aircraft with no passenger seats! A copy of the article is shown overleaf.

The weekly page
that takes the lid off
consumer items

Talking Shop

If you have booked your summer escape to a holiday hotspot, then chances are you are jetting out from one of five key airports. But flying out of the country is the easy bit — often getting to the airport is a minefield of travel options. NIGEL POWLSON checks out the alternatives and the costs.

What happened to the two prototype aircraft? After the suspension of the programme, the second aircraft was flown from Honeywell's plant at Phoenix to join the first aircraft parked against the fence at the Dee Howard facility in San Antonio. Certain cowlings were removed from both aircraft and the second aircraft had its Honeywell advanced flight deck instrumentation removed. They were left there for some time, looking rather forlorn - see photographs below taken on a rare wet day in San Antonio.

Abandoned! The two Dee Howard prototypes.

The first prototype was eventually broken up but the second prototype's fuselage was moved again and was still intact in 1997.

CHAPTER EIGHT

Romania's BAC One-Elevens

As mentioned in the first chapter, the Romanian Government had signed an agreement with British Aerospace in 1979 to produce Spey-powered One-Elevens's under licence in Romania, under the brand name ROMBAC One-Eleven. The first aircraft so produced - from a kit of parts - entered service with the Romanian national airline TAROM, in late 1982.

The Romanians, and in particular the Romanian Aircraft Factory, expressed an interest in fitting the Tay engine on their BAC One-Eleven aircraft, then under construction, as long ago as early 1983. In fact in May that year, as noted earlier, the Director-General of the Romanian Foreign Trade Company, CNA, had written to Rolls-Royce Board Member, Don Pepper, requesting discussions to commence on the conversion of the existing Spey Licence Agreement to a Tay Agreement. This was at a time when the Tay engine had only just been launched on its first application, the Gulfstream IV executive jet. Thenceforth the option of Tay power began to be mentioned by the Romanians in marketing activity with the claim that FAA certification of a Tay-powered Romanian One-Eleven aircraft would be achieved in late 1987.

By late 1987 the Romanians had exhausted their supply of CAA certificated Spey engines for the production programme, but Rolls-Royce was reluctant to supply more engines until certain debts had been paid off. The prospect of expanding the agreement to allow a Romanian One-Eleven -500/Tay programme to be certificated with the Dee Howard Company, using engines supplied through Dee Howard seemed a way out of the impasse. Again, as mentioned earlier, the Dee Howard Company had tried to facilitate this activity by drawing in GPA, the leasing company, as possible customer and the Continental Grain Company of New York, which could arrange finance and was involved in counter-trade activity in Bucharest. However, the ability of the Romanians to pay Dee Howard Co's expected $13m development and certification charges seemed doubtful.

As well as GPA, the newly-formed company, Swift Aviation, was interested in marketing the Tay-powered ROMBAC One-Eleven 500 Series aircraft. When GPA withdrew its interest in dealing with the Romanians, Swift Aviation's view of this withdrawal at the time was that *"the GPA formula makes considerable investment demands on the manufacturer which the economic structure of Romania makes impossible"*. Swift Aviation felt that its own concept, described in Chapter Three, in which Swift itself would supply production materials to the Romanian factory, was more sympathetic to Romania's needs.

Early in 1988 Swift Aviation, later called Associated Aerospace, emerged as serious participants in the Romanian One-Eleven/Tay programme and I have covered Swift's subsequent activities in earlier chapters.

Romania after the Associated Aerospace project

After the collapse of the Swift Aviation/Associated Aerospace project in February 1991, the Romanian Aircraft Factory was on its own again and urgently thinking how to try to revive the One-Eleven/Tay concept. By this time the aircraft factory had adopted the name Romaero and the engine factory had shortened its earlier name to Turbomecanica.

A parallel activity which took place at this time involved Alenia of Italy, which was desperately trying to widen the appeal of its Dee Howard One-Eleven re-engining programme by bringing in other manufacturers. By so doing it was hoping to attract some R&D money to offset the spiralling certification costs on the Dee Howard programme. Alenia was interested in selling a licence in the One-Eleven re-engine business to the Romanians, but felt uncomfortable about dealing with the Romanians direct. Accordingly, the company opened discussions with Israeli Aircraft Industries (IAI) - which had reasonable relations with Romania - to see if the company was interested in managing and marketing a Romaero One-Eleven programme. The Israelis listened politely but were rather dubious as to whether there was any potential market, despite claims by Alenia that Ryan Air and Dan-Air would be likely customers. They were really more interested in joining with Alenia to gain access to European new aircraft programmes which were then being considered.

Re-launch of the Romanian One-Eleven programme

Notwithstanding Alenia's separate attempts to kick-start the Romanian programme, the Romanian Government and Romaero formally announced that they were seeking to re-launch the One-Eleven production programme (with the adoption of Tay power) and asked British Aerospace for assistance in preparing a business plan. However, an independent survey of the potential market at about this time suggested that there was only a limited market for Tay-powered, new production ROMBAC aircraft, perhaps 25 aircraft at most. BAe's preliminary Business Plan only looked viable in the short term if production was limited to the 12 as yet un-built airframes for which the Romanians already had 70% of the parts.

A major meeting about re-activating the programme was held in London in September between BAe, Rolls-Royce and Alenia. BAe, led by Airbus Division Managing Director Chris Geoghagen, advised that a 16-person management team would be required in Bucharest to execute a One-Eleven/Tay certification and production programme. Romanian production aircraft number 409 (which had already flown with Speys) was proposed for the certification programme and BAe suggested that the certification flying should take place in Italy. Alenia claimed that its costs for joining this activity would be $50m. This included the transfer of experience from the Dee Howard re-engining programme (alleged to be worth $35m), certification of the -500 Series aircraft and the supply of three ship-sets of nacelles and thrust reversers. Rolls-Royce declined to sell engines direct to Romaero unless financing was guaranteed or insured by the Export Credit Guarantee Department (ECGD). However, due to political uncertainties at this time in Romania, business with that country was not under ECGD cover.

In late November 1991, General Eugeniu Smirnov, Director General of Romaero visited Rolls-Royce, Company Headquarters, for discussions with BAe and Rolls-Royce on the re-launch proposal. One of Smirnov's concerns was a general lack of knowledge about the position of Alenia and the provision of nacelles and thrust reversers to Romaero. It was discovered that there had been no dialogue between Romaero and Alenia for a year! There was no mention of the suspension of the Dee Howard re-engining programme, or the litigation which had just been announced.

General Smirnov claimed to have a statement from the Romanian Government that it would offer financial guarantees to support the programme - but there was nothing in writing. The Romanians then took the initiative of approaching the newly-formed European Bank of Reconstruction and Development (EBRD) to arrange a meeting on the project. This relatively new international bank, based in London's new Docklands redevelopment area, had been especially formed to invest in those East European countries which had emerged independent, but in many cases impoverished, from the disintegration of the communist bloc. However, the Bank explained that it would not lend more than 35% of the amount required and this would be at market rates. It was also EBRD policy with loans *"to put its money in last and get it out first"*. The Bank queried what investment the manufacturers, particularly BAe and Rolls-Royce, were proposing to make in the Romanian programme. The EBRD was not impressed with the negative answer it received.

Still trying to make some progress, in June 1992, the Romanians approached Charterhouse Bank in London to try to find a way through the financing obstacles. In connection with this, BAe estimated that its costs of certifying the ROMBAC One-Eleven with Tays would be $23m. Though still not having any sort of agreed programme, the Romanians asked Rolls-Royce for a commercial proposal to supply 60 Tay 650 engines.

At the close of 1992, Romaero SA announced a new management team which included:

Tudorel Dumitrascu	-	Managing Director
Dumitru Cucu	-	Production Director
Constantin Dinischiotu	-	Sales & Marketing Director

The Kiwi order

The prospects for a Romanian Tay/BAC One-Eleven programme seemed to be considerably improved by the surprise announcement on 7 February 1993 that Romaero had signed an agreement to build 11 Tay-powered BAC One-Eleven's plus five options, for Kiwi International Airlines. This was a relatively new-start US domestic airline based at Newark, New Jersey. The first two aircraft were expected to be delivered in late 1994. British Aerospace and Rolls-Royce were totally unaware of this new development. How had it come about? Who had put the deal together? In view of all the previous problems, from where was the financing of this deal to come?

It quickly became apparent that the entrepreneur behind this agreement was a little-known aviation financial consultant named Philip Bloom, who lived near Kiwi's operating base. It is possible that he had been approached by the expatriate Romanian community in New York/New Jersey and he already had connections with the newly-established Kiwi management. The attraction for Kiwi was that it was offered the aircraft for USD 18.5m each - a lower price allegedly than it would have to pay for other new 100-seaters - and given the rights to market the aircraft in the Americas. Bloom claimed that the Romanian Government was fully backing Romaero and prepared to guarantee the proposal with state guarantees. A little-known Danish Bank called Unibank, which had leased to Kiwi its first four Boeing 727s, was alleged to be involved. Kiwi was not committed to paying any deposits to Romaero on its purchase but amazingly, for a company and country in such dire financial straits, Romaero purchased a tranche of Kiwi stock and was given a seat on Kiwi's Board.

At first glance, the Kiwi deal, if it had substance, offered the one thing that most previous Romanian ambitions had not had - a significant launch order which should then make commercial financing easier to obtain. In essence the proposal was to complete the build of those remaining 11 BAC One-Eleven aircraft of the batch of 22 which had been licensed by British Aerospace and supplied in kit form and build another five totally new aircraft. The aircraft would be -500 series aircraft and have 104 seats. The engines would be Tay Mark 650-14s and there would be new avionics from Collins and new interiors designed by AIM of Bournemouth.

It was intended that the first two aircraft would be delivered in November and December 1994, with delivery of one aircraft per quarter thereafter, ie a 21-22 month programme to entry into service. The new aircraft was even given a new name and designation, viz, AIRSTAR 2500. (The existing Romanian Spey-powered aircraft was designated BAC One-Eleven -560 Series.) The intention was that the eleventh One-Eleven aircraft on the existing production line, which was already part-built to the extent of having the engine pylons in place, would be used as the prototype for development and certification flying.

After the initial euphoria of the February announcement and a flurry of meetings between Romaero, British Aerospace, Rolls-Royce and Philip Bloom, the first problems started to emerge. Some of these problems were capable of being worked by programme management, prompt decisions and a will to overcome obstacles. I list a few, as follows:

* BAe, the design authority, already had two certification experts in Bucharest, whose job it was to approve the construction of the existing aircraft. However Romaero had not been keeping up with the contracted payment for these services and BAe was on the point of withdrawing its personnel. This would make development and certification of the re-engined aircraft significantly more difficult.

* Although in principle Romaero had kits of parts to build a total of 22 One-Eleven aircraft, ie including the 11 for Kiwi, there were a number of missing items. For example, in February 1993 there were only two sets of undercarriage castings remaining in Bucharest. The lead time on such castings was of the order of 18 months. Also a number of suppliers of One-Eleven systems components had gone out of business.

* No contact appeared to have been made by the entrepreneur or Romaero with the Dee Howard Company, supplier of the nacelles and thrust reversers for the One-Eleven re-engine programme, or Dee Howard's parents, Alenia. There was no knowledge of what reaction they might have to this potential business. In fact, at this time, Alenia was taking legal action against British Aerospace over the termination of the re-engine programme.

Financing the Kiwi proposal

By far the biggest concern was the financing of the project - a matter which had bedevilled previous attempts by the Romanians to launch a programme. Two things became apparent at an early stage of the 'launch'. In March the Danish Bank, Unibank, which had been mentioned by Philip Bloom, declared a loss of $737m on its 1992 operations, the second year in a row of losses. It was judged not to be a serious provider of funds for this project. Further it became clear that Kiwi International Airlines had not only no commitment to put down deposits with its order but, as a start-up carrier, had got its hands full trying to gain market share with its existing Boeing 727 operations.

Philip Bloom attempted to deal with the financial problem by trying to draw together the interested parties and establish a teaming arrangement, involving Romaero, BAe, Rolls-Royce, Philip Bloom & Associates and FLS Aerospace, whose Lovaux Division of Hurn Airport, near Bournemouth, was well-established in overhauling BAC One-Eleven aircraft. FLS Aerospace, led by Peter Purdy, was nominated as the potential team leader to manage the programme. However, BAe and Rolls-Royce were apprehensive that this teaming vehicle would suck them into arranging finance and having to guarantee such finance in the event of programme failure.

A further complication, as mentioned above, was that Alenia/Dee Howard, which would need to be involved to provide its Tay nacelles and thrust reversers, was involved in legal action with British Aerospace. Alenia refused to meet the Romanians and Philip Bloom in the same room as BAe. During this time, Romaero indicated that it was intending to re-design the aircraft structure (for Tay propulsion) in Romania, thus avoiding having to pay royalties to the Dee Howard Company for use of the engineering designs that it had developed for the re-engine programme.

By April, and while the teaming arrangements were still being considered, Philip Bloom tried to arrange, firstly, a bridging loan to get the programme started and also a longer term financial package. He claimed that his efforts were not being helped by the major suppliers (BAe and Rolls-Royce) not appearing with him before the financial community. Nevertheless meetings between Bloom and the Romanian Government had again indicated strong Government support - but nothing in writing. The BAe team, led by Roy Daymond, and Rolls-Royce, led by Ralph Land, indicated that full Government guarantees were mandatory. (Both companies' unstated position was that under no circumstances would they become guarantors if the programme collapsed). At a big meeting at Rolls-Royce headquarters, Capt Iverson, the Chairman of Kiwi, pointedly observed to the Romanian Ambassador in London, Sergiu Celac, that it was the Romanians and its aircraft industry which would get most benefit out of this programme and ought to back it to the hilt and not vacillate.

Lloyds Bank, which had been previously involved with Romanian financing and had been drawn into the discussions, was not comfortable with the Business Plan which Philip Bloom had prepared. BAe and Rolls-Royce likewise considered that the plan seriously underestimated some certification expenses and this undermined the project's viability. An independent review of the project by respected US aircraft valuation expert Morten Beyer advised that the price proposed for the new aircraft looked competitive in the market but also warned that certifying the aircraft to both Federal Aviation Regulations and European regulations was likely to be very time-consuming and expensive. The question was raised, would the Romanian Government guarantee a plan which had every indication of making a loss on the first 11 aircraft?

At about this time, the European Bank of Reconstruction and Development was again approached to back the project. It might have been thought that this institution would have been ideally placed and motivated to back any attempt to rebuild the Romanian aircraft industry but the EBRD took a pessimistic line on the project and even the Romanian delegate on the bank's council appeared unsympathetic. EBRD's principal concern was that Kiwi's 11 aircraft order was not an adequate guarantee of the long term viability of Romaero.

At the beginning of May (1993) Philip Bloom attempted to call a major meeting in London for the CEOs of BAe, Rolls-Royce and FLS Aerospace, the banks and the EBRD, together with the Romanian Minister of Finance. While this was in preparation, Peter Purdy, CEO of FLS Aerospace, resigned. FLS was in the middle of a major re-organisation and downsizing and subsequent to Purdy's departure showed an ever-decreasing interest in the AirStar project. BAe was also showing signs of diminished support for the Romaero programme and it was suspected that the discussions then ongoing with Taiwan Aerospace over the continued development of the rival BAe 146 (Avro RJ) aircraft were a factor in this.

The May 19/20 meetings exposed that financing was still the major obstacle. Lloyds Bank continued to be interested in the concept but made clear that insurance of the financing would have to be provided by the Export Credit Guarantee Department (ECGD) and pointed out that the sum required for this (Romaero) deal alone exceeded the amount of cover recently allocated by ECGD to the whole of Romania. Promising noises continued to be heard from time-to-time from the Romanian Government about its willingness to support the programme, but nothing ever came of this.

As mentioned in the previous chapter, a potentially important meeting occurred on 15 June when the Managing Directors of Rolls-Royce Aerospace Group (John Sandford), British Aerospace, Airbus Division (Bob

McKinlay) and Alenia (Nino d'Angelo) and their supporting staffs held a meeting at the Paris Air Show. This was primarily about trying to re-activate the Alenia/Dee Howard One-Eleven -2400 re-engine programme and little reference was made to the Romaero programme. Rolls-Royce agreed to make a financial concession towards the re-start of the re-engine programme but made it conditional on BAe supporting the Romaero programme and the Romanians signing purchase orders for 22 Tay 650 engines. (Rolls-Royce and Romaero had already initialled a purchase contract for these engines on 11 June). These conditions were not well received by BAe and a period of disagreement ensued - and no action.

As a consequence of the withdrawal of FLS Aerospace from programme involvement, Romaero approached the Marshall Company of Cambridge. The latter initially expressed interest in exploring the possibility of working with the Romanians but subsequently withdrew, telling the Romanians that it had been 'warned off' by another party from getting involved.

End of ROMBAC Spey programme

A major blow to the whole programme occurred on 7 July 1993 when British Aerospace, through its Manager for Romania, Garry Bishop, finally withdrew the last two of its representatives at the Romaero factory, reportedly scrapping their records and files as they did so. Press articles at the time reported that this action stemmed from the fact that Romaero owed BAe somewhere between $5m and $10m in unpaid licence fees.

The effect of BAe's withdrawal was that licence production of the ROMBAC One-Eleven aircraft (with Spey engines) ceased. The photograph below shows the unfinished, tenth Romanian-built Spey-powered BAC1-11 on the production line, at the time of cessation. Somewhat late in the day, the National airline TAROM announced that it wished to re-engine with Tays its existing fleet of One-Eleven aircraft. At the same time Philip Bloom was still trying to put together a bridging loan of $25m (with terms acceptable to the Romanians) and had engaged the US company Bankers Trust to go to the syndication market. However, BAe was reported to be only willing to support the programme if full-term financing was in place, ie not just a bridging loan. However, in September Bankers Trust notified the parties that it had withdrawn its interest in the programme, citing the disappointing attitude of the EBRD, the lack of financial support by Rolls-Royce and BAe and the fact that no senior officials of BAe were willing to meet the Bankers Trust party that visited the UK.

In the last quarter of 1993 the chances of the programme being launched became less and less. The Dee Howard Company offered to Romaero the

Uncompleted Romanian One-Eleven, airframe number 410

fuselage of second re-engined prototype (s/n 076) without engines or cowls for $6.5m. Romaero was not able to find that sort of cash but came back with an optimistic proposal of a joint venture company of the Alenia/Dee Howard and Romaero to undertake a certification programme for -400 Series and -500 Series aircraft, for both new aircraft production and re-engining of existing aircraft. This was not taken up.

From then on, a number of interested parties investigated the possibility of re-starting the programme but without BAe interest and no visibility of any financial support, the Romanian dream of their production One-Eleven aircraft with new, more powerful, modern technology engines, finally died. The rather belated journal news item below, reproduced by permission of *Flight International*, records the end. (Note, as described earlier, that Rolls-Royce had no intention of allowing Tay engines to be licence-produced in Romania. No Tay powerplants were produced by Turbomecanica for Romaero. The last paragraph of *Flight International's* article is wishful thinking by the journal's Romanian news source!)

Romaero admits defeat on One-Eleven launch

ROMANIAN AIRCRAFT manufacturer Romaero has given up a longstanding ambition to manufacture upgraded, re-engined One-Eleven airliners for the world market.

The Bucharest-based company struggled for years to find the necessary $100 million funding to proceed with the revamped aircraft, known as the Airstar 2500.

A launch order had been placed in 1993 for 11 aircraft and five options from US carrier Kiwi International Airlines. This deal was struck in return for a $1 million investment in Kiwi from Romaero.

Romaero built nine standard, Rolls-Royce Spey-powered, "Rombac" One-Eleven Series 560s from kits supplied by British Aerospace, under a licence acquired from the UK manufacturer in May 1977. These were sold to Tarom and Romavia, with the last aircraft delivered in 1992.

The Rombac One-Eleven programme has reached a dead end

Romaero had initially hoped to begin production of the Airstar 2500 in time to deliver the aircraft to Kiwi in 1995.

The upgraded aircraft was to be equipped with the R-R Tay 650, which improved performance and efficiency by 20%. The Airstar was also to have a Honeywell "glass" cockpit. Romaero's plans were further hampered by the termination of Dee Howard's One-Eleven Tay re-engineing programme, which it planned to use for the upgrade.

The Tays were to be licence-produced by Bucharest-based engine manufacturer Turbomecanica. In the end, Turbomecanica produced two powerplants which were delivered to Romaero, but only to be subsequently sold on as spare parts. ❏

FLIGHT INTERNATIONAL 2 - 8 April 1997

Reflections

At the close of what should have been a viable and attractive project, one is left to reflect, what went wrong? Why didn't the Tay-powered One-Eleven become a successful programme? Could something different have been done to rescue the concept? On the other hand, and with respect to the re-engining programme, were there times when it would have been prudent for the Dee Howard Company or Aeritalia/Alenia to have pulled out before losing large sums of money?

It is the author's opinion that, from mid-1983, when corporate BAe started to get involved in what had, up to then, been a Weybridge project, the Tay/One-Eleven concept had a struggle to survive. Most commentators were of the opinion that BAe viewed the Tay/One-Eleven as something which might diminish the business prospects of its 146 airliner.

For Mr Dee U Howard, the One-Eleven re-engining project looked very sensible and fitted in nicely with his company's skills in modifying aircraft. However, reports of the protracted negotiations between Dee Howard, Ian Munro and British Aerospace to sign a Technical Assistance Agreement suggest that BAe did not proceed with any urgency or particular enthusiasm and the talks seemed to drag on interminably. From Dee Howard's first interest to programme launch took two years. Arguably with a willing partner the process of tying up an agreement could have been achieved in a few months.

Progress after launch was equally slow. Possibly the uneven release of funding by the Dee Howard Company, to continue the design and development programme, was a reason for the protracted timescale. It is also a factor that engineering staff were diverted from time-to-time during this critical period, to prepare the case for Dee Howard's ambitions to undertake other re-engining programmes. What also seems clear is that the programme needed a 'strong-arm' Programme Director properly to manage the programme and maintain a tight timescale.

Was there a case for Aeritalia to stop the re-engining programme when it took over Dee Howard in 1988-89? Possibly, but remember that Aeritalia wanted to expand its aircraft modification activities outside its Italian home base and the re-engine programme was exactly the type of programme which suited the company's expansion plans.

Another occasion when Aeritalia might have decided that it could cut its losses was January 1991, when it was obvious that none of the six marketing initiatives in 1990 had succeeded. By then, five years after programme launch, confidence was ebbing among the aircraft community that the re-engined One-Eleven would ever be certificated.

Some may say, should Rolls-Royce have offered some financial support or advantageous terms to help secure more sales for this further application for the Tay engine? The Company would almost certainly have replied, *'No'*. Rolls-Royce regards itself as a supplier to the trade. This means that it could not be seen to be supporting one customer (Dee Howard) without similarly supporting Fokker and Gulfstream Aerospace. In other respects, the Company supplied engineering support in its customary professional manner, but on the commercial side, it seemed to the author that its dealings in the later stages became increasingly 'hard-nosed'.

Reflecting on the whole Dee Howard episode one feels that it might have had more chance of success if

(a)   the early programme had been better managed, more securely financed and had employed some vigorous and empowered marketeers

(b)   the time from launch to first flight had been reduced from three years to say, 18-24 months.

There would then have been a good prospect for early orders, the whole programme would have looked much healthier and could have gained a new momentum.

Of the other proposals, Derek Lowe's was a brave attempt to build on sensible ideas for a UK re-engining programme but he really needed the support of a credible project team and the sustained backing of some 'big hitters' to make any progress with British Aerospace. Such a team ought to have been formed and broken surface in early 1984, before the BAe - Dee Howard negotiations became exclusive.

The Associated Aerospace concept could have worked, but it appears that AAe underestimated the true costs of the programme and not understood the nature of trying to do business in Ceaucescu's Romania. Finding backers to finance this project - seen by many as somewhat risky - was a continual problem. However, in the end it was the Romanians who effectively terminated the AAe programme. Also, while BAe and Rolls-Royce were willing to go along with the programme, the Romanian project was still going to need nacelles and thrust reversers from Alenia/Dee Howard. These in turn awaited the successful conclusion of the Dee Howard certification programme which had only started in mid-1990. AAe had no opportunity of going to another source, as they debated at the time, because of Dee Howard's exclusive Agreement with BAe.

This brings me to my final thoughts - what about the Romanians? Having established the Spey/One-Eleven Agreement in the late 1970s there was clearly much enthusiasm in the Romanian aircraft industry both for keeping production going, but also substituting the Tay for the Spey. But all attempts failed. These included the GPA/Dee Howard/Continental Grain initiative, the Associated Aerospace programme and finally the Philip Bloom/Kiwi scheme. All of them needed some tangible evidence that the Romanian government was going to stand behind the various proposals with government guarantees. This was most starkly apparent in the middle of the Kiwi discussions, where all signs pointed to a need for the government to give its guarantee, but despite repeated 'warm words', nothing ever emerged.

The country was certainly in a desperate financial position at the time. One assumes that it was a government concern to try to make sure that any default would fall back on to the western manufacturers, not itself. Unfortunately, the latter had learnt the lessons from the earlier stages of the ROMBAC programme to avoid exposure! Perhaps the European Bank of Reconstruction and Development could have spent less money on its own administration and beautifying its headquarters building and put some seed money into supporting this attempt by a struggling Romanian industry to get on its feet.

In conclusion, this is a sad story and a disappointing end to a programme which offered so much promise.

And what of the two main components of this tale, the BAC One-Eleven aircraft and the Rolls-Royce Tay engine? One-Eleven production (with the Spey engine) finally ceased in 1993 when BAe withdrew its certification staff from the Romanian Aircraft Factory. The aircraft has continued in service, but in diminishing numbers and is increasingly branded as a very noisy and 'dirty' aircraft. The surviving fleet, world-wide, is believed to be about 90 aircraft. At the time of going to print, an American company which had for years been trying to develop a viable Stage 3/Chapter 3 hush kit is understood to have finally achieved American FAA certification for the -400 series aircraft. This will save some aircraft from enforced retirement but unfortunately these aircraft will have none of the advantages of much-improved performance, noise compliance with clear margins and low emissions of a Tay re-engined aircraft.

As for the engine, the Tay has turned out to be one of Rolls-Royce's most successful programmes. The Fokker 100, Fokker 70 and Boeing 727-100 re-engining applications have now closed but the current version, the Tay 611-8 for the Gulfstream IV, is expected to continue in production until about year 2003. Around 1800 engines have been manufactured so far. During 2000, Gulfstream Aerospace signed a contract for an improved version of the Tay 611, which is expected to continue in production until at least the end of the decade.

APPENDIX I

The Tay engine and the BAC One-Eleven: chronology

Year	Dee Howard Co	Romania	Other events
1982		First flight, ROMBAC Spey/One-Eleven	
1983		Romanian interest in Tay/One-Eleven	Tay launched (GIV) BAe offer letter to operators
1984	Dee Howard Co negotiations with Salem Binladen, BAe, Rolls-Royce		
1985			
1986	Dee Howard programme launched		Tay 610 and 620 certificated
1987			Gulfstream IV certificated; Fokker 100 EIS
1988	Salem Binladen's fatal accident; Aeritalia buys 40% of Dee Howard		Tay 650-15 (Fokker 100) certificated Fo 100 (Tay 650) EIS
1989	Aeritalia takes over Dee Howard	Swift Aviation signs with Romania; Pres. Ceaucescu executed	Tay 650-14 (1-11) cert
1990	First re-engined aircraft flies	Associated Aerospace launches Romanian programme	GPA rules out major order; Aeritalia becomes Alenia
1991	Second aircraft flies; Re-engine prog ends	Collapse of Associated Aerospace	
1992			Tay 651 (727RE) cert B727-100RE EIS
1993		Kiwi programme launched; Kiwi programme end	

Tay One-Eleven: "British industry should be involved"

SIR—The editorial and the article "Tay One-Eleven agreements unfurl", in Flight for December 6, made fascinating reading, but the statements made therein have only served to increase doubt, and not to dispel confusion.

The editorial speaks of Dee Howard's "exclusive" agreement with British Aerospace to re-engine the One-Eleven. Yet in Dee Howard's own detailed release the word "exclusive" is significantly absent.

Six months after the Dee Howard contract was signed, the managing director of British Aerospace's Civil Aircraft Division stated: "I neither shut the door or left it open on any possibility of Tay One-Eleven and One-Eleven propfan activity in the UK". From Rolls-Royce's statement in the article, it appears that they reserve the right to talk to anyone showing interest in re-engining One-Elevens. Both positions indicate a less than "exclusive" situation.

The initial retrofit contracts for executive One-Eleven owners gave Dee Howard the unilateral right to terminate the programme if it did not receive at least 15 confirmed orders accompanied by deposits. There appears to be only one American executive One-Eleven operator interested in Tay conversion at this time.

Since Dee Howard has neglected to make a clear statement to Flight International as to how many commitments they have received since January 1986, we can only assume that the current commitments are minimal. I hasten to add that over a year ago my company forecast that this portion of the retrofit market had serious commercial faults if tackled in accordance with Dee Howard's original concepts.

The only correct environment in which to launch the One-Eleven Tay is within Britain, since 22 per cent of the British jet airliner fleet consists of One-Elevens. The airlines are motivated by two ministers: by Michael Spicer MP regarding aircraft noise reduction, and by John Moore MP regarding increased competition. The One-Eleven Tay, as well as being the cheapest stage III noise certificated aircraft, would fly faster, higher, and much farther than any other existing 100-seat aircraft with competitive operating economics.

There is sufficient British airline interest in retrofitting British Aerospace's most successful jet airliner to assure commercial viability, correctly configured. There is also a 4,000 n.m. corporate jet within the design, with a cabin to match the range. I for one, cannot see why Britain needs a small American company to fit British engines to British airframes for use by British airlines. Or is British manufacturing now only excited by the De Loreans and Learfans of this world?

The Romanian licenced manufacturer clearly needs a viable Tay retrofit programme to regenerate its ailing One-Eleven production line which, after belated delivery of a set of seven One-Elevens to Tarom, is suffering an extremely severe case of post-natal manufacturing depression. The ongoing viability of the Romanian One-Eleven programme is important to the many British manufacturers involved, and to long-term Anglo-Romanian relations.

It is apparent that British Aerospace does not wish to lead such a programme, especially after failing to mention the existence of the One-Eleven and its Romanian production line in their privatisation prospectus.

I believe that the Department of Trade and Industry should be actively promoting and seeking the involvement of British industry in the Tay One-Eleven project. The Government should encourage such activity, as it would assist in improving East-West relations, would reduce airport noise, would allow the One-Eleven airline owners to remain competitive for decades to come, and would give Rolls-Royce more engine orders before privatisation. Such a process seems entirely compatible with this Government's declared policy.

Is it not appropriate to start resolving this matter in what is left of Britain's declining Industry and Energy Efficiency Year?

DEREK LOWE
Director
Executive Jet Sales
70 High Street
Newport Pagnell
Buckinghamshire MK16 8AQ

FLIGHT INTERNATIONAL, 27 December 1986

APPENDIX III

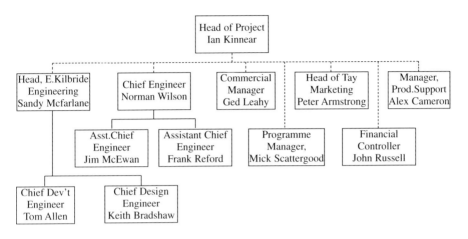

Tay Project Management, Mid-1988

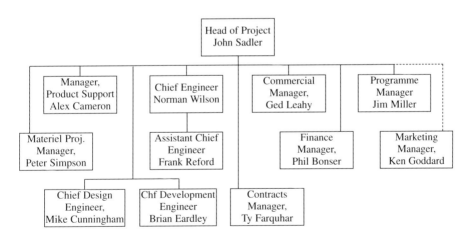

Tay Project Management, November 1990

INDEX

The Historical Series is published as a joint initiative by the Rolls-Royce Heritage Trust and The Sir Henry Royce Memorial Foundation.

Also published in the series:

No 1   Rolls-Royce - the formative years 1906-1939
         Alec Harvey-Bailey, RRHT 2nd edition 1983

No 2   The Merlin in perspective - the combat years
         Alec Harvey-Bailey, RRHT 4th edition 1995

No 3   Rolls-Royce - the pursuit of excellence
         Alec Harvey-Bailey and Mike Evans, SHRMF 1984

No 4   In the beginning - the Manchester origins of Rolls-Royce
         Mike Evans, RRHT 1984

No 5   Rolls-Royce - the Derby Bentleys
         Alec Harvey-Bailey, SHRMF 1985

No 6   The early days of Rolls-Royce - and the Montagu family
         Lord Montagu of Beaulieu, RRHT 1986

No 7   Rolls-Royce - Hives, the quiet tiger
         Alec Harvey-Bailey, SHRMF 1985

No 8   Rolls-Royce - Twenty to Wraith
         Alec Harvey-Bailey, SHRMF 1986

No 9   Rolls-Royce and the Mustang
         David Birch, RRHT 1997

No 10   From Gipsy to Gem with diversions, 1926-1986
         Peter Stokes, RRHT 1987

No 11   Armstrong Siddeley - the Parkside story, 1896-1939
         Ray Cook, RRHT 1989

No 26   Fedden - the life of Sir Roy Fedden
           Bill Gunston OBE FRaeS, RRHT 1998

No 27   Lord Northcliffe - and the early years of Rolls-Royce
           Hugh Driver, RREC 1998

No 28   Boxkite to Jet - the remarkable career of Frank B Halford
           Douglas R Taylor, RRHT 1999

No 29   Rolls-Royce on the front line - the life and times of a Service
           Engineer
           Tony Henniker, RRHT 2000

Special   Sectioned drawings of piston aero engines
           L Jones, RRHT 1995

Monograph Rolls-Royce Armaments
           D Birch, RRHT 2000

Technical Series

No 1   Rolls-Royce and the Rateau Patents
           H Pearson, RRHT 1989

No 2   The vital spark! The development of aero engine
           sparking plugs
           K Gough, RRHT 1991

No 3   The performance of a supercharged aero engine
           S Hooker, H Reed and A Yarker, RRHT 1997

No 4   Flow matching of the stages of axial compressors
           Geoffrey Wilde OBE, RRHT 1999

Books are available from:
Rolls-Royce Heritage Trust, Rolls-Royce plc, Moor Lane, PO Box 31,
Derby DE24 8BJ